D1492313

MARY FORD

# THE BEGINNERS
## — GUIDE TO —
# CAKE
# DECORATING

## BCA
LONDON · NEW YORK · SYDNEY · TORONTO

# AUTHOR

Mary Ford stresses the importance of all aspects of cake artistry, but gives special emphasis to the basic ingredients and unreservedly recommends the use of Tate and Lyle Icing Sugar.

Colour backdrops supplied by Robert Horne Paper Company Limited, Eastleigh, Hampshire.

© Copyright 1992 Mary Ford Publications Limited.
This edition published 1992 by BCA by arrangement with Mary Ford Publications Limited, 294b Lymington Road, Highcliffe-on-Sea, Christchurch, Dorset BH23 5ET, England.

**CN 8482**

Typesetting by Avant Mode Limited, Bournemouth.
Printed and bound by Vincenzo Bona - ITALY
ISBN 0 946429 38 3

Mary Ford's unrivalled skill and infinite patience make her a superb teacher of her craft. Mary has been passing on her expertise for over two decades, through personal contact with students and in her books. During that time she has gained a world-wide reputation for skill and imagination combined with common sense and practical teaching ability. Her unique step-by-step approach, with the emphasis on numerous colour illustrations and brief editorial advice, is ideally suited for introducing beginners to the skills of cake artistry.

Mary's husband, Michael, collaborates with Mary in planning and producing her books. All the photographs are taken by him in their studio in Highcliffe. He is also editorial director for the books.

Mary Ford acknowledges with grateful thanks the assistance of Betty Nethercott in making some of the wedding cakes in this book. Some of the cakes in this book have been featured in previous Mary Ford books.

MARY FORD

# CONTENTS

Note: when making any of the recipes in this book, follow one set of measurements only as they are not interchangeable.

# INTRODUCTION

I genuinely believe that anyone can learn and, most importantly, enjoy the art of cake-making and decorating. I have designed this book specially for the beginner – although the more experienced decorator will still find plenty of ideas to fire the imagination. Whether you are a young mother wanting to surprise and delight your child, an older mother desiring to make a wedding cake for her daughter, a grandmother celebrating her 40th wedding anniversary, or a cake-maker seeking inspiration for a special cake, you will find all you need set out in easy pictorial stages.

Some of the designs are so simple that a complete novice can begin immediately, and yet they are stunningly effective. The ingenious use of ribbons can add impact, and decorating aids such as doyleys make creating intricate patterns extremely simple. The busy cake maker can make use of ready-made products such as 'instant' icing, sugarpaste or almond paste to speed up the process of covering the cake, and ornaments or artificial flowers can be purchased to add the finishing touches.

The book, which is a carefully structured course, opens with a section introducing basic techniques of cake making and decorating. Reading through this section, with its advice on how to achieve the best results, will quickly familiarise you with the special terms applicable to cake artistry. These terms are explained fully in the Index/Glossary at the back of the book. The Index also lists cakes under headings such as 'Birthday', 'Wedding', etc, for ease of reference. Each decorating section also has an introductory page, which should be read before commencing work.

My aim has been to de-mystify the art and to communicate in clear, simple language all the information you need to develop your skills. This is complemented by the step-by-step photographs which illustrate every stage of the process. The introductory section also contains my own hints and tips for perfect results.

It is well worth practising the basic skills – an upturned cake tin, for instance, provides an excellent base on which to practice piping, and a buttercream-coated sponge makes a wonderful teatime treat. Then, when you come to decorate a cake for a special occasion, you will have developed your skills and confidence – confidence is one of the most important assets a cake decorator can have. Many of the designs, however, need no skill at all.

Following the basic section, you will find a whole host of designs for every possible occasion and every level of experience and, as your skills develop, you will not only be able to tackle more complex cakes, all fully illustrated in the step-by-step photographs, but may also be inspired to combine elements from different cakes into your own unique creation. The sense of satisfaction you will receive from creating your own special cakes is reward enough, but the delighted surprise of the recipient adds immeasurably to the pleasure. Even after all my years of professional experience, I still treasure the moment when I hand over a cake.

I hope that this book will kindle your enthusiasm for cake making and decorating and that you will pursue your interest by looking at other books in my step-by-step series.

# EQUIPMENT

The right equipment makes cake decorating much easier, but it is possible to improvise and many of the items required will already be in your kitchen. It is worth buying the best quality equipment as this will not rust, bend or chip, and may last a lifetime with careful use. Always ensure equipment is scrupulously clean and free from grease.

Where possible, equipment such as wooden spoons and plastic bowls should be kept specially for icing as they can absorb strong flavours and taint icing. Metal spoons and bowls, other than stainless steel, are not suitable as they may discolour the icing. Glass or earthenware bowls are ideal, provided they have no cracks which can harbour grease or dirt. A mixer is useful for making coverings and coatings.

If intending to decorate cakes frequently, it is worth investing in a turntable. A good turntable will support a heavy cake and will have a minimum diameter of 23cm (9") to enable safe carriage of a loaded 51cm (20") cake board. It must have a non-slip base and should be easy to turn when in use. However, a turntable for small cakes can be improvised with an upturned cake tin or plate.

A good quality, smooth and heavy rolling pin about 45cm (18") will be needed for rolling out pastes, and nylon spacers can be helpful in achieving an even thickness. For modelling flowers, a smaller plastic rolling pin can be useful.

Stainless steel palette knives with firm blades are required for both mixing in colour and for coating cakes. An 18cm (7") and a 10cm (4") knife should be sufficient. A 38cm (15") straight edge is needed for

smoothing royal icing or buttercream. This can be made of stainless steel or rigid plastic, and can be improvised with a stainless steel ruler. The sides of a cake can be smoothed using a palette knife, but purpose-made side scrapers make the task easier. Scrapers for cakes should be fairly rigid and are usually plastic.

Instructions for making a greaseproof paper piping bag are given on page 29 and this is recommended for all icing. Piping tubes, which can be plastic or metal, are readily available and shapes are illustrated in the Index/Glossary and indicated in the text by (No.   ). Tubes should always be thoroughly washed immediately after use to remove icing before it hardens.

Much of the remaining equipment required, such as skewers, measuring jugs, nylon sieves, etc, and additional items such as a pair of compasses and fine paintbrushes may well be in your home already. However, all the tools and equipment in this book are obtainable from the Mary Ford Cake Artistry Centre, 28-30 Southbourne Grove, Bournemouth, Dorset BH6 3RA, England, or local stockists.

## DESIGN

When selecting a cake, the size and shape is important. A heart-shaped cake would be ideal for an engagement, wedding or valentine cake, and any unusual shape adds impact to a simple design. A square or round cake is, however, suitable for any occasion. The size of cake will depend upon the number of guests and the table on page 12 shows approximately how many portions each size of fruit cake will provide.

Once the shape has been chosen, a design appropriate to the occasion or to the interests of the recipient should be selected. Hobbies are always a useful theme for birthday cakes, and young children enjoy cakes featuring their favourite toys or story book characters. Personalising a cake is a simple matter of adjusting wording or decoration.

## COLOUR

Colouring cakes is easy and a carefully chosen shade will enhance the finished result. Always ensure that sufficient icing or sugarpaste is coloured to complete the work as it is difficult to match colours later. Various shades of edible food colouring are available, which can be added to icing, sugarpaste or almond paste, and coloured piping gel is an instant decorating medium. Always remember that icing dries a little darker than at first appears. When pale colours are used, the effect should be delicate and not washed-out. Toning or contrasting shades of icing, and the use of two colours together for the piping, can be extremely effective. If a really brilliant shade is introduced, in a flower spray for example, this should be kept to a minimum. A splash of colour can, however, add a focal point and children enjoy bright colours.

## TEMPLATES

Templates are used for transferring designs onto the cake. All the templates in this book can be easily changed in size, if necessary, using an enlarging photocopier.

Templates are usually traced onto thin card and cut out, or traced onto grease-proof paper using a food-approved pen. A card template can then be piped around with royal icing (the template being removed when the icing is dry), or be scratched around with a sharp-pointed tool as required. If a template is to be used as the base for a run-out (see p.47), waxed paper should be taped over the template. If the paper template is to be used for transferring a design onto the cake, it can be positioned and then pressed through by use of a sharp-pointed tool. Alternatively, retrace on the back with a food-approved pen, then turn over and position on the cake. Trace again using a food-approved pen.

# ALL-IN-ONE SPONGE

## RECIPE TABLES

| SPONGE TIN SHAPES | SPONGE TIN SIZES | | | | | |
|---|---|---|---|---|---|---|
| ROUND | 15cm (6") | 18cm (7") | 20.5cm (8") | 23cm (9") | 25.5cm (10") | 28cm (11") |
| SQUARE | 12.5cm (5") | 15cm (6") | 18cm (7") | 20.5cm (8") | 23cm (9") | 25.5cm (10") |
| PUDDING BASIN | 450ml ($^3$/4pt) | 600ml (1pt) | 750ml (1$^1$/4pt) | 900ml (1$^1$/2pt) | 1 litre (1$^3$/4pt) | 1200ml (2pt) |
| Self raising flour | 45g (1$^1$/2oz) | 60g (2oz) | 85g (3oz) | 115g (4oz) | 170g (6oz) | 225g (8oz) |
| Baking powder | $^1$/4tsp | $^1$/2tsp | $^3$/4tsp | 1tsp | 1$^1$/2tsp | 2tsp |
| Soft (tub) margarine | 45g (1$^1$/2oz) | 60g (2oz) | 85g (3oz) | 115g (4oz) | 170g (6oz) | 225g (8oz) |
| Caster sugar | 45g (1$^1$/2oz) | 60g (2oz) | 85g (3oz) | 115g (4oz) | 170g (6oz) | 225g (8oz) |
| Fresh egg | 45g (1$^1$/2oz) | 60g (2oz) | 85g (3oz) | 115g (4oz) | 170g (6oz) | 225g (8oz) |
| Baking temperature | 170°C (325°F) or Gas Mark 3 | | | | | |
| Baking time (approximately) | 20 mins | 25 mins | 30 mins | 32 mins | 35 mins | 40 mins |
| NOTE: | Baking time may need to be increased slightly for cakes baked in a pudding basin | | | | | |

**BAKING TEST** When the sponge has been baking for the recommended time, open the oven door slowly and, if sponge is pale in colour, continue baking. When the sponge is golden brown, draw fingers across the top (pressing lightly) and, if this action leaves an indentation, continue baking. Repeat test every 2-3 minutes until the top springs back when touched.

**STORAGE** The sponge may be wrapped in waxed paper and deep-frozen for up to 6 months. Use within 3 days of baking or after defrosting.

**PORTIONS** A 20.5cm (8") sponge will provide approximately 16 portions.

This sponge is ideal for children's cakes or teatime treats as it is easy to make and has a light texture when baked. It should be eaten within 2-3 days but freezes well.

## INGREDIENTS for TWO 20.5cm (8") round sponges.

See page 10 for ingredients of other tin sizes.

| | |
|---|---|
| Self-raising flour | 170g (6oz) |
| Baking powder | 1½ level tsp |
| Soft (tub) margarine | 170g (6oz) |
| Caster sugar | 170g (6oz) |
| Fresh egg | 170g (6oz) |

## Chocolate sponge:

For a chocolate sponge, replace 30g (1oz) of flour with 30g (1oz) of cocoa powder in the recipe.

## ITEMS REQUIRED

2 round sponge tins 20.5cm (8")
Greaseproof paper and butter
Wire cooling tray

**Bake** at 170°C (325°F) or gas mark 3 for approximately 30 minutes.

**BAKING TEST** see page 10

**STORAGE** see page 10

**1** Grease tins with butter and line the bases with greased greaseproof paper.

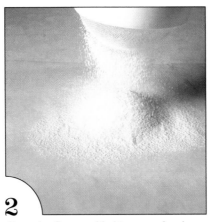

**2** Sieve the flour and baking powder three times to ensure a fine consistency.

**3** Place all the ingredients together in a mixing bowl.

**4** Beat the ingredients together for 3-4 minutes, until thoroughly mixed and of a light consistency.

**5** Divide the mixture evenly between the prepared tins. Bake in the pre-heated oven for approximately 30 minutes. Test before removing – see page 10.

**6** After baking, leave the sponges in the tins for 5 minutes before turning out onto a wire cooling tray.

# FRUIT CAKE

**RECIPE TABLES**

| CAKE TIN SHAPES | CAKE TIN SIZES | | | | | |
|---|---|---|---|---|---|---|
| ROUND | 15cm (6") | 18cm (7") | 20.5cm (8") | 23cm (9") | 25.5cm (10") | 28cm (11") |
| SQUARE | 12.5cm (5") | 15cm (6") | 18cm (7") | 20.5cm (8") | 23cm (9") | 25.5cm (10") |
| Self raising flour | 100g (3½oz) | 145g (5oz) | 200g (7oz) | 225g (8oz) | 315g (11oz) | 400g (14oz) |
| Ground nutmeg | pinch | ¼tsp | ½tsp | ½tsp | ¾tsp | 1tsp |
| Ground mixed spice | ¼tsp | ½tsp | ½tsp | ¾tsp | 1tsp | 1½tsp |
| Ground mace | small pinch | small pinch | medium pinch | medium pinch | large pinch | large pinch |
| Sultanas | 85g (3oz) | 130g (4½oz) | 170g (6oz) | 215g (7½oz) | 285g (10oz) | 340g (12oz) |
| Currants | 85g (3oz) | 130g (4½oz) | 170g (6oz) | 215g (7½oz) | 285g (10oz) | 340g (12oz) |
| Raisins | 85g (3oz) | 130g (4½oz) | 170g (6oz) | 215g (7½oz) | 285g (10oz) | 340g (12oz) |
| Glacé cherries | 45g (1½oz) | 65g (2¼oz) | 85g (3oz) | 105g (3¾oz) | 145g (5oz) | 170g (6oz) |
| Mixed peel | 45g (1½oz) | 65g (2¼oz) | 85g (3oz) | 105g (3¾oz) | 145g (5oz) | 170g (6oz) |
| Lemon zest (lemons) | ¼ | ½ | ½ | 1 | 1½ | 2 |
| Ground almonds | 22g (¾oz) | 30g (1oz) | 45g (1½oz) | 50g (1¾oz) | 75g (2½oz) | 85g (3oz) |
| Soft (tub) margarine | 85g (3oz) | 130g (4½oz) | 170g (6oz) | 215g (7½oz) | 285g (10oz) | 340g (12oz) |
| Soft light brown sugar | 85g (3oz) | 130g (4½oz) | 170g (6oz) | 215g (7½oz) | 285g (10oz) | 340g (12oz) |
| Fresh egg | 85g (3oz) | 130g (4½oz) | 170g (6oz) | 215g (7½oz) | 285g (10oz) | 340g (12oz) |
| Rum | ½tbls | ½tbls | 1tbls | 1tbls | 1½tbls | 2tbls |
| Black treacle | 1tbls | 1tbls | 1½tbls | 1½tbls | 2tbls | 3tbls |
| Baking temperature | 150°C (300°F) or Gas Mark 2 | | | 140°C (275°F) or Gas Mark 1 | | |
| Baking time (approximately) | 1½ hrs | 1¾ hrs | 2 hrs | 2½ hrs | 3 hrs | 3½ hrs |

**BAKING TEST** At the end of the recommended baking time, bring the cake forward from the oven so that it can be tested. Then insert a stainless steel skewer into the centre of the cake and slowly withdraw it. The skewer should be as clean as it went in. This means the cake is sufficiently baked. If cake mixture clings to the skewer, remove the skewer completely and continue baking at the same temperature. Test thereafter every 10 minutes until the skewer is clean when withdrawn from the cake.

**STORAGE** When the cake is cold carefully remove from the tin, then remove the greaseproof paper. Wrap the cake in waxed paper and leave in a cupboard for three weeks to mature.

**PORTIONS** To calculate the estimated number of portions that can be cut from the finished cake, firstly add together the total weight of the cake ingredients, almond paste, sugarpaste or/and royal icing to be used. An average cut piece of finished cake weighs 60g (2oz) therefore divide accordingly.

**Approximate portions:**

| Round cakes | Portions | Square cakes | Portions |
|---|---|---|---|
| 13cm (5") | 14 | 13cm (5") | 16 |
| 15cm (6") | 22 | 15cm (6") | 27 |
| 18cm (7") | 30 | 18cm (7") | 40 |
| 20.5cm (8") | 40 | 20.5cm (8") | 54 |
| 23cm (9") | 54 | 23cm (9") | 70 |
| 25.5cm (10") | 68 | 25.5cm (10") | 90 |
| 30cm (12") | 100 | 30cm (12") | 134 |

| Tiered cakes | Round cakes | Square cakes |
|---|---|---|
| 2-tier 18 & 25.5cm (7 & 10") | 98 | 130 |
| 3-tier 15, 20.5, 25.5cm (6, 8, 10") | 130 | 171 |
| 3-tier 13, 18, 23cm (5, 7, 9") | 98 | 126 |

Fruit cake makes an ideal base for both sugarpaste and royal iced celebration cakes, and it is the traditional medium for wedding cakes as it has excellent keeping properties. Timing is important when making a fruit cake, as it needs at least three weeks to mature before use.

## INGREDIENTS for 20.5cm (8") round or 18cm (7") square cake.

| | |
|---|---|
| Self-raising flour | 200g (7oz) |
| Ground nutmeg | ½ teaspoon |
| Ground mixed spice | ½ teaspoon |
| Ground mace | medium pinch |
| Sultanas | 170g (6oz) |
| Currants | 170g (6oz) |
| Raisins | 170g (6oz) |
| Glacé cherries | 85g (3oz) |
| Mixed peel | 85g (3oz) |
| Lemon | zest of ½ |
| Ground almonds | 45g (1½oz) |
| Soft (tub) margarine | 170g (6oz) |
| Soft light brown sugar | 170g (6oz) |
| Fresh egg | 170g (6oz) |
| Rum | 1 tablespoon |
| Black treacle | 1½ tablespoons |

## ITEMS REQUIRED

Round cake tin 20.5cm (8")
x 7.5cm (3") deep
Greaseproof paper and margarine
Wire cooling tray

**Bake** at 150°C (300°F) or gas mark 2 for approximately 2 hours.

**BAKING TEST** see page 12

**STORAGE** see page 12

See page 12 for ingredients of other cake tin sizes.

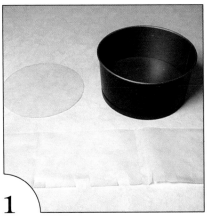

**1** Cut greaseproof paper 5cm (2") deeper than the cake-tin to cover inside. Cut along bottom edge 2.5cm (1") up at intervals. Cut a circle for the base.

**2** Brush the inside of cake tin with soft margarine.

**3** Cover the side with the greaseproof paper then place the circle into the bottom. Brush the greaseproof paper with margarine.

**4** Carefully weigh all the ingredients separately. Chop the cherries in half. Clean and then remove any stalks from the fruit.

**5** Grate the lemon. Mix fruit together with the rum in a bowl. Leave all ingredients overnight in a warm place 18°C (65°F).

**6** Sieve the flour, nutmeg, spice and mace together three times.

**7** Place all the ingredients, except the fruit, into a mixing bowl.

**8** Beat together for approximately 2 minutes on high speed to form a batter.

**9** Stir in the fruit, using a large spoon, until all the fruit is mixed into the batter.

**10** Spread mixture into prepared cake tin. Place tray of hot water at bottom of pre-heated oven. Then place cake in centre of oven.

**11** Remove water halfway through baking time. Continue baking. If necessary cover the cake-top with paper. Test after recommended baking time – see page 12.

**12** When baked remove cake from oven and leave in the tin on a wire tray for 24 hours. See page 12 for storage instructions.

# ALMOND PASTE

Almond paste differs from marzipan in that almond paste is a mixture of uncooked ground almonds, sugar and glucose or eggs, whereas marzipan is made from cooked ground almonds and sugar. Either paste is suitable for covering cakes. Almond paste can be stored in food-approved polythene or in a sealed container in a cool, dry place. Do not overmix the paste and never allow almond paste to come into contact with flour.

| **INGREDIENTS (recipe 1)** | | **INGREDIENTS (recipe 2)** | |
|---|---|---|---|
| Icing sugar | 170g (6oz) | Icing sugar | 225g (8oz) |
| Caster sugar | 170g (6oz) | Caster sugar | 225g (8oz) |
| Ground almonds | 340g (12oz) | Ground almonds | 445g (16oz) |
| Glucose syrup | 225g (8oz) | Egg yolks | approximately 6 |

**1**
Carefully sieve the icing sugar twice.

**2**
Place the dry ingredients into a mixing bowl and stir together using a hook shaped beater.

**3**
For recipe 1, warm the glucose syrup in a separate bowl in hot water.

**4**
Pour the warmed glucose syrup, or egg yolks, into the dry ingredients.

**5**
Mix all the ingredients together until a pliable paste is formed. Add more glucose syrup, or egg yolks, if necessary.

**6**
Store in a sealed food-approved polythene bag, with the date it was made, until required.

# BUTTERCREAM

Buttercream is an ideal medium for coating children's cakes as it is easily coloured and flavoured. To vary the taste and texture of buttercream beat in any of the following: whisked egg white, milk, egg, marshmallow, fondant, condensed milk, and edible colours and flavourings. To obtain the best results, always use fresh butter at a temperature of 18-21°C (65-70°F).

**INGREDIENTS**

| | |
|---|---|
| Butter | 115g (4oz) |
| Icing sugar | 170-225g (6-8oz) |
| Warm water | 1-2 tablespoons |
| Food colouring | |
| Flavouring | |

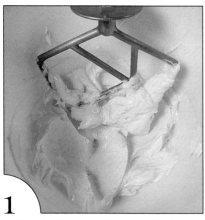

**1**
Soften the butter and beat until it is light and fluffy.

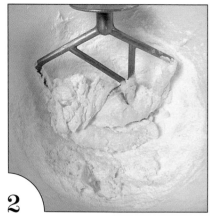

**2**
Sieve the icing sugar and gradually add to the butter, beating well after each addition.

**3**
Add the warm water, and flavouring. Beat the mixture once again.

**4**
Strained fruit juice of choice can be used as a flavouring if desired.

**5**
Add and thoroughly mix in the appropriate food colouring if required.

**6**
For chocolate flavoured buttercream quickly stir in melted chocolate. Use 60g (2oz) of chocolate to 225g (8oz) of buttercream.

# ALBUMEN SOLUTION

When making albumen solution it is essential that all utensils are sterilised and free from grease. When the albumen powder is mixed into the water, it will go lumpy. After 1 hour, stirring occasionally, the lumps will dissolve to form a smooth liquid. Once the solution has been made, it should be kept in a refrigerator in a sealed container. Bring to room temperature before use.

## INGREDIENTS

| | |
|---|---|
| Pure albumen powder | 15g ($\frac{1}{2}$oz) |
| Water | 85g (3oz) |

**1** Pour the water into a bowl and stir whilst sprinkling in the powdered albumen.

**2** Thoroughly mix with the whisk, but do not beat. Leave for 1 hour, stirring occasionally.

**3** Strain the solution through a fine sieve or muslin. It is then ready for use.

# ROYAL ICING

## INGREDIENTS

| | |
|---|---|
| Fresh egg white or albumen solution | 100g ($3\frac{1}{2}$oz) |
| Sieved icing sugar | 455g (16oz) |

**Note:** If using fresh egg whites separate 24 hours before required.

## GLYCERIN – Table for use

For soft cutting royal icing add to every 455g (1lb) of prepared royal icing:
1 teaspoon of glycerin for the bottom tier of a three-tier cake.
2 teaspoons of glycerin for middle tier of a three-tier cake.
3 teaspoons of glycerin for top tier or for single-tier cakes.

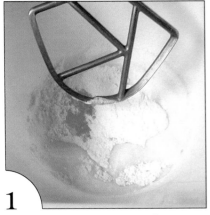

**1** Pour the fresh egg whites or albumen solution into a mixing bowl. Stir in half the sieved icing sugar until dissolved.

**2** Stir in remaining sugar and then clean down the inside of the bowl.

**3** Beat mixture until light and fluffy and peaks can be formed. Scrape down inside of bowl and cover with a damp cloth.

# SUGARPASTE

Sugarpaste is ideal for covering cakes. It is also easily shaped with the fingers for modelling animals, figures and flowers. Colourings and flavourings can be kneaded into the paste, but care should be taken that sufficient quantity is coloured to complete each project. Fix sugarpaste to sugarpaste with pure alcohol, such as vodka or gin; egg white, royal icing or cooled boiled water.

**INGREDIENTS**

| | |
|---|---|
| Water | 2 tablespoons |
| Powdered gelatine | 1½ level teaspoons |
| Liquid glucose | 1½ tablespoons |
| Glycerin | 2 teaspoons |
| Sieved icing sugar | 455g (16oz) |

**Storage:** Sugarpaste should be kept in a food-approved polythene bag in a refrigerator. It will keep for up to 2 weeks. The bag should be clearly labelled with the date it was made. Bring to room temperature before use.

**MODELLING PASTE:** add 2 teaspoons of gum tragacanth to the basic sugarpaste recipe and work well in. Leave for 24 hours before use. Store as for sugarpaste.

**1**
Pour the water into a stainless steel or non-stick saucepan. Sprinkle on the powdered gelatine and dissolve over a low heat.

**2**
Add the glucose and glycerin and stir in before removing the saucepan from the heat.

**3**
Add the icing sugar gradually, mixing continuously with a spoon to avoid any lumps developing.

**4**
Continue adding the icing sugar until it is no longer possible to stir the mixture.

**5**
Remove the spoon and add the remaining icing sugar by kneading the mixture between fingers and thumb.

**6**
Continue kneading the paste until clear and smooth. The paste is then ready for use. See above for storage.

# FLOWER PASTE

Flower paste is a firm, sweet paste which produces a life-like translucent finish, ideal for modelling flowers. The paste dries very quickly so it is important to cut only a small piece at a time when using, and the bulk should be re-sealed. A small piece will go a long way when rolled out very thinly. Each piece of paste should be worked well with the fingers before use in order to achieve the right texture. If it is too hard or crumbly, add a little egg white and white fat to make it more pliable and slow down the drying process. Moisten and fix flower paste with egg white or cooled, boiled water.

## INGREDIENTS

| | |
|---|---|
| Sieved icing sugar | 455g (16oz) |
| Gum tragacanth | 3 teaspoons |
| Cold water | 5 teaspoons |
| Gelatine | 2 teaspoons |
| White vegetable fat | 2 teaspoons |
| Liquid glucose | 2 teaspoons |
| Egg white | 1 (size 2) |

**Storage:** Place in a food-approved polythene bag and store in an airtight container in a refrigerator before use. Bring to room temperature before use.

**Accessories** such as wires, stamens and tapes are available from cake decorating suppliers.

**1**
Mix the icing sugar and gum tragacanth together then sieve into a bowl. Place bowl over a saucepan of boiling water and cover with a cloth and plate. Heat gently until sugar is warm.

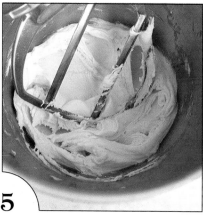

**2**
Pour the water into a cup. Sprinkle on the gelatine and leave for 10 minutes until spongy. Place cup in a saucepan of hot water (not boiling) until the gelatine dissolves.

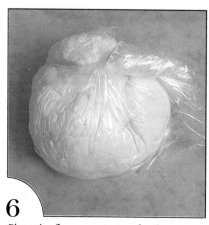

**3**
Add the white fat and glucose to the melted gelatine and heat gently until dissolved.

**4**
Separate the white from the yolk of egg and remove the 'string'.

**5**
Add all ingredients to the warmed icing sugar. Beat for approximately 15-20 minutes until white and stringy.

**6**
Place the flower paste in a food-approved polythene bag and store in a sealed container in a refrigerator for a minimum of 24 hours before use.

# LAYERING AND COATING A SPONGE

**1**
Remove the top crust from two sponges. Upturn and remove the bottom crust.

**2**
Place one sponge on a cake board and cover the top with jam or preserve. Place second sponge on top.

**3**
Place on a turntable. Cover the sponge-top with buttercream, rotate the turntable as you work, and smooth with a palette knife.

**4**
Spread buttercream around the side of the sponge with a palette knife.

**5**
Smooth the side whilst rotating turntable. Remove surplus buttercream from the top-edge. Place in a refrigerator for 1 hour and coat again if required.

**6**
**Alternative coating patterns**
Apply a second coat of buttercream to cake top. Draw a serrated scraper across one half of the top in a zigzag motion.

**7**
Apply a second coat of buttercream to the cake-side and hold a serrated scraper firmly against the side. Rotate the turntable.

**8**
Coat the cake-side with buttercream. Move the scraper in waves, whilst turning the turntable, to produce a zigzag effect.

**9**
Coat the cake-side with buttercream. Hold the coated cake in palm of hand. Fill other hand with roasted nibbed almonds and palm onto cake-side until evenly covered.

# DECORATED SPONGES

**1**

Prepare the sponge by following steps 1-5 on page 20.

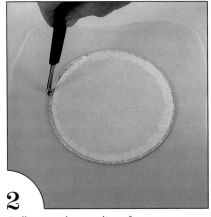

**2**

Roll out and cut a disc of sugarpaste to match the size of the coated sponge (using a cake card as a guide).

**3**

Remove the surplus sugarpaste and slide the cake card under the disc.

**4**

Now remove the disc from the cake card by sliding it directly in position on the sponge-top.

**5**

Cover sponge side with chopped nuts or other covering of choice.

**6**

Decorate sponge with sugarpaste hearts and then a personal message (No.1).

**7**

For an alternative design make and fix a sugarpaste flower, then pipe stem (No.2) and leaves with a leaf bag (see p.45) leaving space for message of choice.

**8**

A decorated top displaying piped storks (No.2) and cut-out sugarpaste flowers.

**9**

Simple, effective designs can be achieved by using sugarpaste cut-outs, fixed with royal icing.

# COVERING A CAKE-TOP WITH ALMOND PASTE

Almond paste or ready-made marzipan can be used to cover a cake. Always ensure that the layer is thick enough to prevent the cake from discolouring the icing.

It is important to prepare the cake properly before covering by removing the top of a dome-shaped cake or filling in any imperfections with almond paste. Ensure that the sides are straight and properly square. Any burnt fruit should be removed.

Almond paste should be rolled out on an icing or caster sugar dusted surface. Never use flour or cornflour as this could cause fermentation.

Apricot purée is the most suitable fixing agent as it has least colour and flavour. This should be boiled before use and brushed on immediately.

The covered cake should be left to stand in a dry room 18°C (65°F) for 24 hours before decorating. Never store a covered cake in a sealed plastic container.

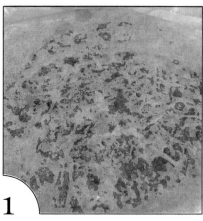

**1**
It is advisable to use a cake which has matured (the outside of the cake is then moist). This usually takes two to three weeks after the cake has been made.

**2**
Remove the waxed paper, place the cake upside down onto a board and brush brandy or rum over the surface (1 teaspoon per 455g (1lb) of cake).

**3**
Using icing sugar for dusting, roll out almond paste between spacers to achieve an even thickness.

**4**
Cut the almond paste into a disc the same size as the cake-top using a cake tin base or template as guide.

**5**
Thinly spread boiled apricot purée over the almond paste, then upturn the cake onto the almond paste, as shown.

**6**
Upturn the cake and place onto a cake card or board. Wrap side in waxed paper. Leave to dry for 24 hours before decorating.

# COVERING A CAKE
# WITH ALMOND PASTE

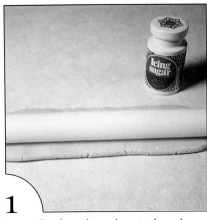

**1**
**Round cake:** Almond paste the cake-top (see p.22). Roll out, onto icing sugar, one piece of almond paste three times the diameter of the cake.

**2**
Cut the strip of almond paste to approximately the depth of the cake.

**3**
Spread boiled apricot purée over the strip of almond paste.

**4**
Fix the almond paste to the cake side, using flat of the hand and cut to correct length.

**5**
Trim the surplus from the cake-top edge, keeping the knife close to the surface. Leave to dry 3 days before coating with royal icing.

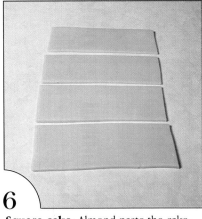

**6**
**Square cake:** Almond paste the cake-top (see p.22). Roll out and cut four strips of almond paste, the same size as the cake side.

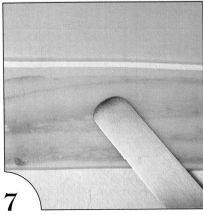

**7**
Spread boiled apricot purée over each strip.

**8**
Press each strip firmly to the cake sides, as shown.

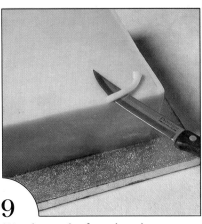

**9**
Trim the surplus from the cake-top edge, keeping the knife close to the surface. Leave to dry 3 days before coating with royal icing.

# COVERING A FRUIT CAKE
# WITH SUGARPASTE

**1**

Fill in the cake-top imperfections with small pieces of almond paste and then brush boiled apricot purée over the whole cake-top and side.

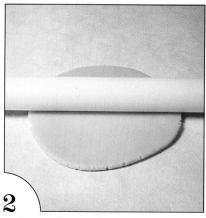

**2**

Roll out sufficient almond paste to cover the entire cake.

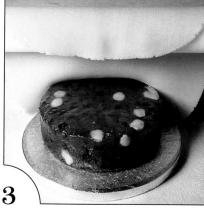

**3**

Place the almond paste over the rolling pin and slowly unroll it onto the cake, as shown.

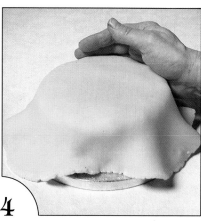

**4**

Lightly press and smooth the almond paste against the cake surface to expel any trapped air.

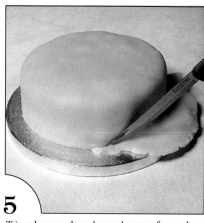

**5**

Trim the surplus almond paste from the cake-base, keeping the knife tight against the cake-side. Leave to dry for 24 hours.

**6**

Brush clear alcohol (e.g. gin or vodka) over the almond paste.

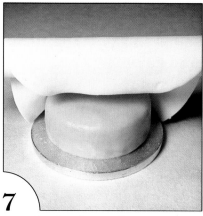

**7**

Immediately roll out sufficient sugarpaste (made 24 hours before use) and place over the cake, using the rolling pin as shown.

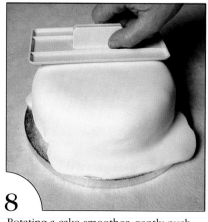

**8**

Rotating a cake smoother, gently push the sugarpaste onto the cake to flatten the surface.

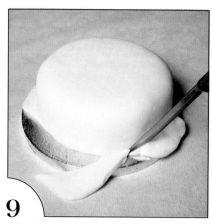

**9**

Trim the surplus sugarpaste from the cake-base keeping the knife tight against the cake-side.

# COATING CAKES WITH ROYAL ICING

Royal icing is the traditional medium for coating celebration cakes and its beautiful, smooth finish is perfect for formal piped designs. Ready-to-mix and ready-made royal icings are now available which are ideal for the absolute beginner to work with as they are extremely easy to apply and ensure a good result.

Getting as good a shape as possible at the almond paste stage will make coating easier. Always ensure that the top is flat and the sides vertical as this enables a smooth layer of icing to be laid down. The almond paste covered cake should be left for at least 24 hours before coating.

To produce a good finish, it is essential that care should be taken when making the icing, and when coating, as the slightest lump will mar the smoothness. All items used in preparation, coating and decorating should be scrupulously clean.

Icing for coating should be made 24 hours in advance and stirred immediately before use to disperse any bubbles. The consistency should form soft peaks and a drop of water can be added if the icing is too stiff to spread easily. A very small amount of blue colour can be added to improve the whiteness but blue should not be added to icing which will be coloured further. A table for the addition of glycerin to produce soft-cutting royal icing is on page 17.

The icing should be stored in a closed container and a small amount transferred to a separate bowl, covered with a damp cloth. The icing should be kept well scraped down to prevent drying out.

A stiff, stainless steel palette knife is ideal for spreading the royal icing and a stainless steel ruler can be used for flattening and levelling the top surface. When using side scrapers, the fingers should be spread across the width of the scraper to ensure an even pressure when rotating the turntable. It is preferable for the cake to have at least three thin coats, each coat being allowed to dry before applying the next. When using coloured icing, the first coat should be white, the second a pale shade of the colour required, and the third coat the actual colour. Coloured icing will dry patchy unless evenly applied.

When the covering is complete, the cake should be left to stand overnight in a warm room 18°C (65°F) before decorating. Do not store a coated cake in a sealed plastic container.

As royal icing is a form of meringue, it must be well beaten as otherwise the icing is heavy and difficult to handle. Under-mixed icing has a slightly creamy look and should be beaten further. Over-beating the icing, in a high speed mixer for instance, incorporates too much air and causes the icing to become fluffy. If the icing sugar is added too quickly, then the icing becomes grainy in appearance. Correctly made royal icing has a clean, white colour and is slightly glossy and light in texture.

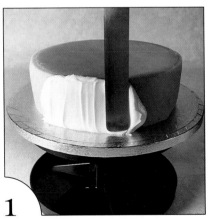

**1** **To coat a round cake:** Place the cake with board onto a turntable. Using a palette knife, spread royal icing around the cake side.

**2** To smooth, hold a scraper against the cake-side and rotate the turntable one complete turn. Repeat until smooth.

**3** Remove the surplus royal icing from the cake-top and board, using a palette knife. Leave to dry for 12 hours.

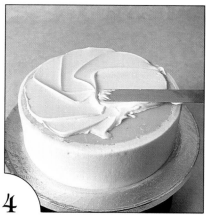

**4** Spread royal icing evenly over the cake-top using a paddling movement with a palette knife.

**5** Level the icing using a stainless steel rule in a backwards and forwards motion over the cake-top until smooth.

**6** Remove the surplus icing from the edge of the cake-top and leave to dry for 12 hours. Repeat steps 1-6 for two more layers.

**7** **To coat straight sided cakes:** Coat opposite sides with royal icing, remove surplus and leave to dry for 12 hours. Repeat until all sides are covered.

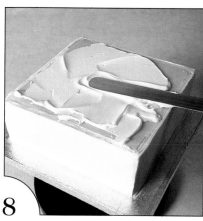

**8** Spread royal icing evenly over the cake-top using a paddling movement with the palette knife.

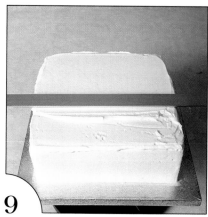

**9** Level the icing using a stainless steel rule in a backwards and forwards motion over the cake-top until smooth.

**10** Remove the surplus royal icing from the edges of the cake. Leave to dry for 12 hours. Repeat steps 7-10 for two more layers.

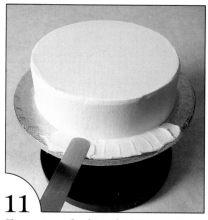

**11** **To coat a cake board:** Using a palette knife, spread royal icing over the cake board surface, as shown.

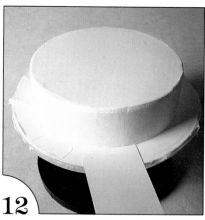

**12** Smooth the royal icing, holding the scraper steady while rotating the turntable. Clean sides. Leave to dry for 12 hours then decorate as required.

# TIERING CAKES

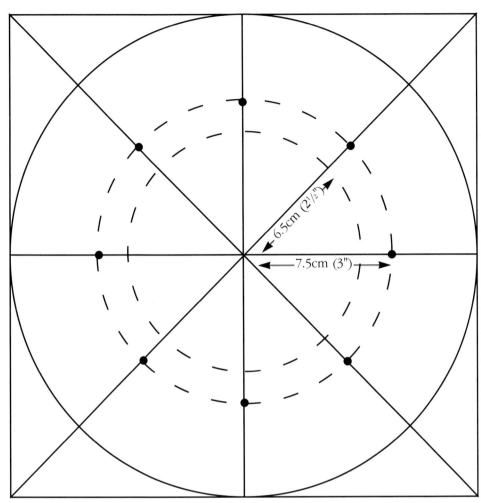

Not to scale

6.5cm (2½")

7.5cm (3")

For a 20.5cm (8") cake, pillars should be positioned 6.5cm (2½") from the centre. For a 25.5cm (10") cake, pillars should be positioned 7.5cm (3") from the centre. A square cake usually has 4 pillars which can be on the diagonal or cross, whichever suits the design best. A round cake usually has 3 pillars in a triangle, or four arranged in a circle.

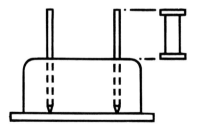

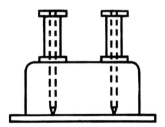

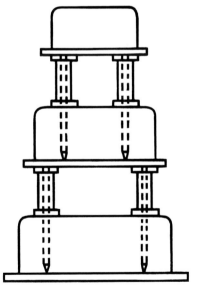

## TIERING A SUGARPASTE-COVERED CAKE

**1**

Push food-approved rods into the cake to the board. Cut rods to height of pillar.

**2**

Place the pillars over the rods.

**3**

Assemble the cake, as required.

# MAKING TEMPLATES

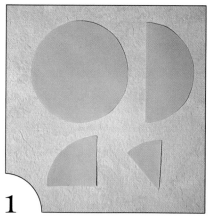

**1**

**Petal template:** Cut a paper circle to the same size as the cake-top. Fold in half, then half again and in half once more.

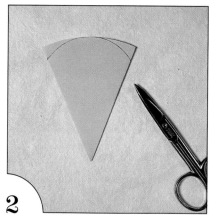

**2**

Mark the paper as shown and, using sharp scissors, carefully cut along the line whilst keeping the paper folded.

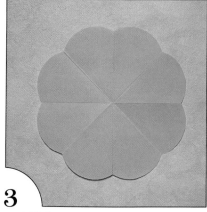

**3**

Unfold the template and check with the picture that it is correct. Place between two flat surfaces to flatten out.

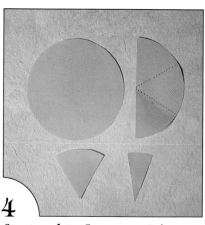

**4**

**Star template:** Cut a paper circle to the same size as the cake-top. Fold in half, then into three and finally in half again.

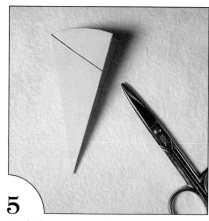

**5**

Mark the paper as shown and, using sharp scissors, carefully cut along the line whilst keeping the paper folded.

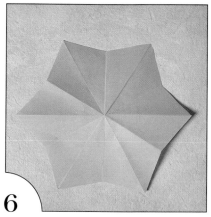

**6**

Unfold the template and check with the picture that it is correct. Place between two flat surfaces to flatten out.

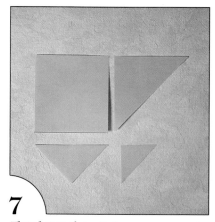

**7**

**Floral template:** Cut a paper square to the same size as the cake-top. Fold diagonally, then in half and in half again.

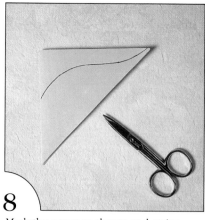

**8**

Mark the paper as shown and, using sharp scissors, carefully cut along the line whilst keeping the paper folded.

**9**

Unfold the template and check with the picture that it is correct. Place between two flat surfaces to flatten out.

# MAKING A PIPING BAG

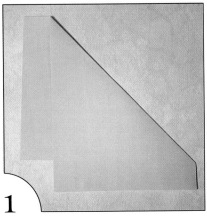

**1**

Size of greaseproof required: Large bags 45.5 x 35.5cm (18 x 14"); Medium 35.5 x 25.5cm (14 x 10"); Small 25.5 x 20.5cm (10 x 8"). Fold as shown.

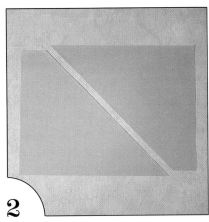

**2**

Cut along the fold line (to form two identical shapes).

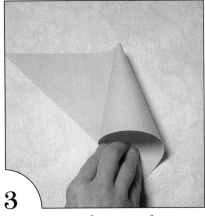

**3**

Turn one piece of greaseproof paper long edge uppermost. Pick up the top right hand corner and start to turn it towards the centre, form a cone.

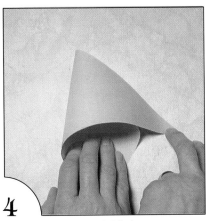

**4**

With the other hand, lift the opposite corner completely over the cone.

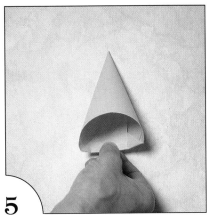

**5**

Continue curling the paper under the cone and pull taut, until a sharp point is formed at the tip.

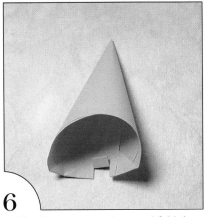

**6**

Fold in loose ends and cut and fold the small section shown to secure the bag.

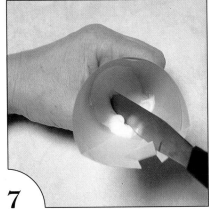

**7**

Cut tip off bag to hold a piping tube. Drop tube in and, using a palette knife, half fill the bag with royal icing or buttercream.

**8**

Flatten the wide part of the bag and gently squeeze filling down to the tube. Fold each side of the bag to the centre.

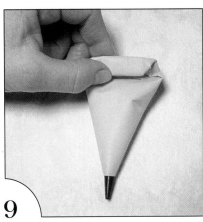

**9**

Roll the wide end of the bag towards the tube to seal the bag. It is then ready for use.

# WRITING

It is useful to develop a distinctive style of lettering, and to practice this until it can be piped and evenly spaced with uniform height as poor lettering can ruin even the most beautiful design. A clear piece of Perspex or glass can be placed over a pattern if using the script for the first time. Once you have mastered the script, begin to practice common inscriptions until you become familiar with how much space each word takes up. You can then count the number of letters in a new word and judge how much space will be required.

Royal icing, without glycerin, should be made the day before it is required. Remove a small portion of royal icing from the mixing bowl and smooth out on a clean surface with a palette knife to remove air bubbles before filling the piping bag.

The cake coating must be dry before attempting to pipe the message. Royal icing piping can be piped directly onto dry royal icing, sugarpaste, marzipan or almond paste, chocolate and fondant. When piping lettering on buttercream, use a paper guide to avoid marking the surface and always chill the cake before working. Ensure that the cake is at a comfortable working height in a dry warm atmosphere. Always work so that you draw the piping bag towards yourself, with the bag aligned to the direction of the stroke.

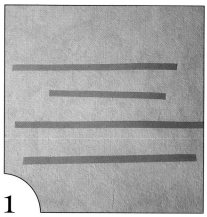

**1**
Cut strips of food approved thin card 6mm (¼") wide to use as guides.

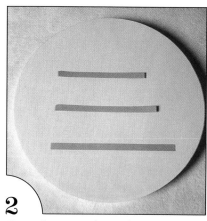

**2**
Cut and position the guides as required onto a dry cake-top.

**3**
Pipe the inscription of choice (No.2). Leave to dry for 1 hour. Then remove the guides.

**4**
Carefully pipe over the writing in a dark coloured royal icing (No.1)

**5**
The cake can be finished with appropriate decorations.

**6**
The guide can be angled and the style of writing varied as appropriate.

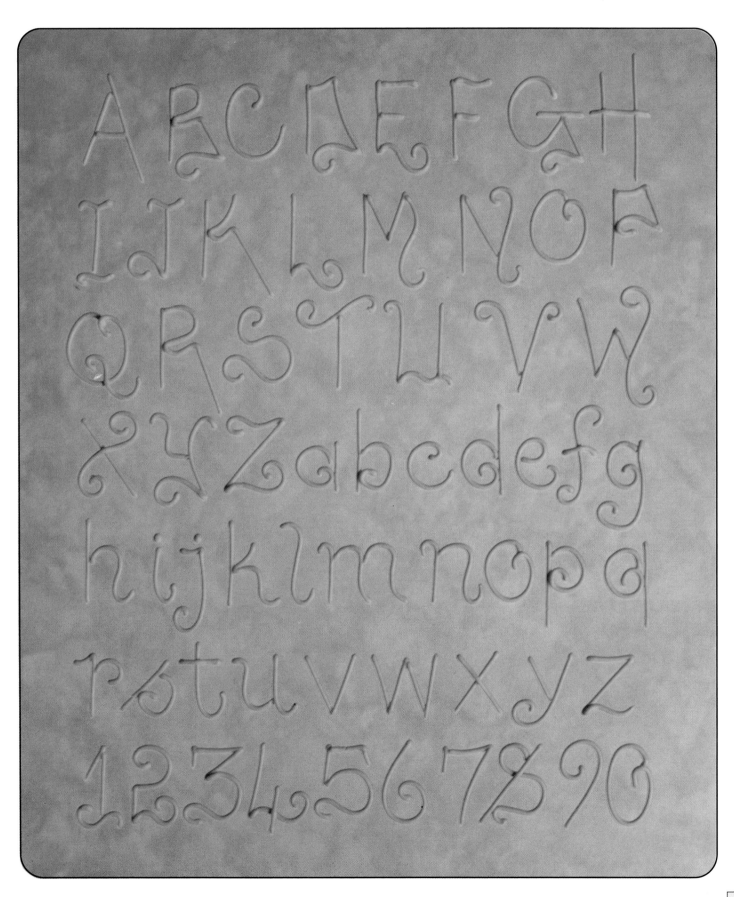

# HOW TO PIPE LINES

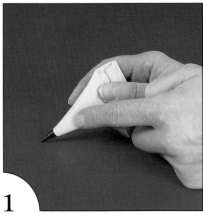

**1**

**How to pipe a straight line:** To steady the tube, use both hands. Touch surface with tube end, keeping bag at the angle shown.

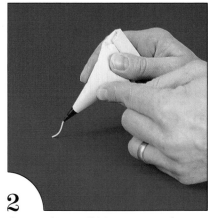

**2**

Squeeze bag until icing appears, then pipe and, at the same time, lift the bag.

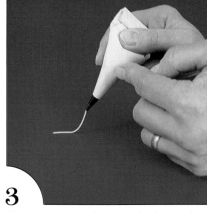

**3**

Continue piping, keeping the bag at the height shown and bringing it towards you.

**4**

Before reaching the end of the line, stop squeezing and start to lower the bag to the surface, keeping the icing line taut.

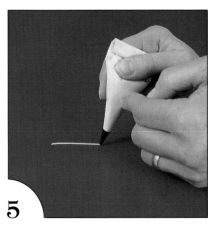

**5**

Continue to lower the bag, bringing it into a more vertical position.

**6**

To finish the line, touch the surface with the tube and pull the tube away, keeping the bag upright.

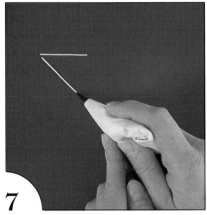

**7**

When piping a diagonal line always bring the tube towards you in the direction of the line.

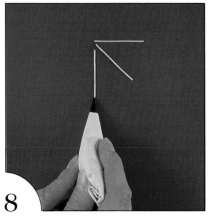

**8**

When piping a downward line always bring the tube towards you in the direction of the line.

**1**

**How to pipe a curved line:** Touch the surface with the tube in a vertical position.

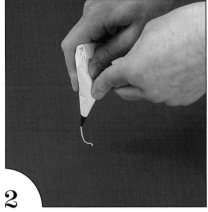

**2**

Squeeze the bag until the icing appears, then pipe and, at the same time, lift the bag.

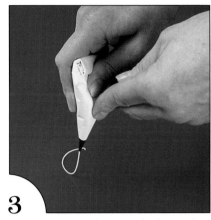

**3**

Continue piping, keeping the bag at the height shown and start to curve the line.

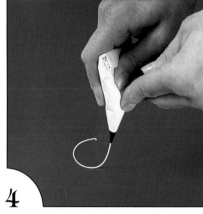

**4**

Before completing the curved line, stop squeezing and start to lower the bag, continuing the curve.

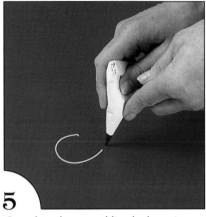

**5**

Complete the curved line by lowering the tube to the surface.

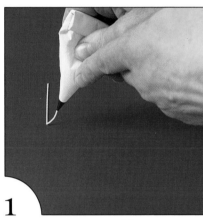

**1**

**Piping various curved lines:** Start to pipe at the base of the straight line and then lift the bag to the height shown.

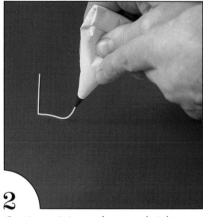

**2**

Continue piping at the same height, curving the line as shown.

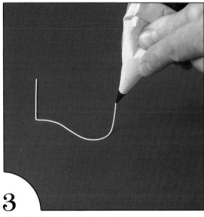

**3**

Gradually lower the tube to create a tighter curve.

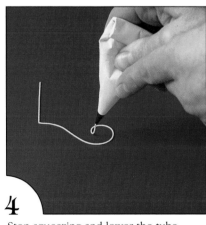

**4**

Stop squeezing and lower the tube, continuing curve.

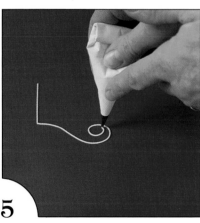

**5**

To complete the curves, touch the surface with the tube and then pull the tube away.

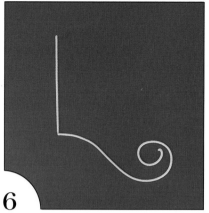

**6**
Picture shows the completed lines.

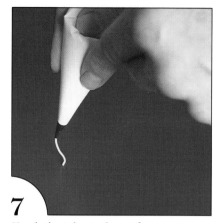

**7**
Touch the tube to the surface, squeeze and immediately lift the bag vertically to height shown.

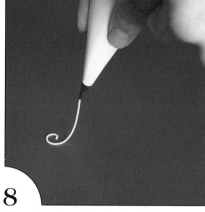

**8**
Move bag in a tight circle whilst continuing piping at the height shown.

**9**
Stop squeezing and lower the tube to the surface, keeping the icing taut.

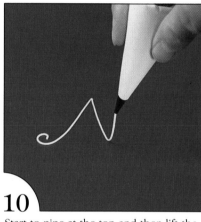

**10**
Start to pipe at the top and then lift the bag to the height shown, curving the line.

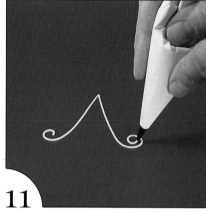

**11**
Continue piping, reducing height. Stop squeezing the bag and touch surface with the tube to complete the curved line.

**12**
Picture shows joined curved lines.

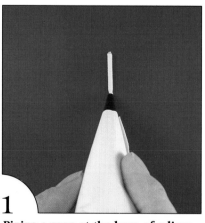

**1**
**Piping a rope at the base of a line:**
Pipe a straight line (see steps 1-5 on p.32) but do not remove the tube.

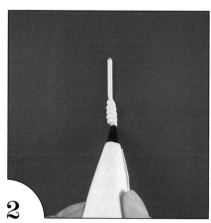

**2**
Move the end of the tube in a clockwise direction, touching the surface on each turn.

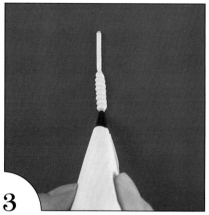

**3**

Continue piping in an even thickness.
Stop squeezing and pull the tube away
at required length.

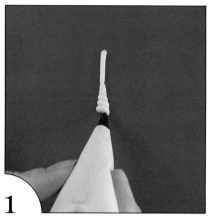

**1**

**Piping a barrel in a line:** Pipe steps
1-2 on p.34, for piping a rope at the
base of a line, but gradually increase the
size of the circles.

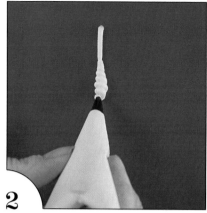

**2**

At the centre of the barrel gradually
decrease the circles so they match the
first half.

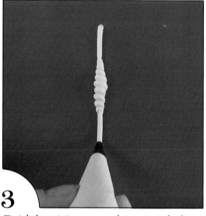

**3**

Finish by piping a matching straight line.
Stop squeezing and pull the tube away.

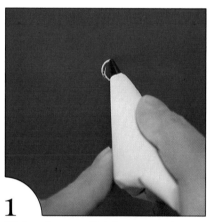

**1**

**Piping tracery:** Lightly squeeze the
piping bag, moving the tube on the
surface in the direction shown.

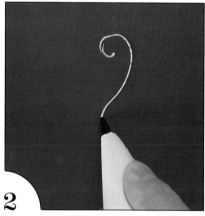

**2**

Continue piping in the direction shown.

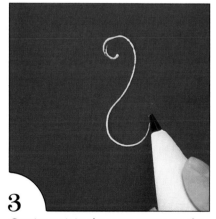

**3**

Continue piping but stop squeezing the
bag just before completing the line.

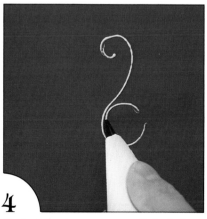

**4**

Re-start the tracery in an anti-clockwise
direction.

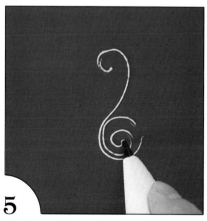

**5**

Continue piping to form a spiral line to
the centre. Stop squeezing the bag and
pull away.

**1**

**Piping on the side of a cake:** Tilt the cake on a heavy support.

**2**

Pipe the top of the "J", or letter of choice, keeping the tube close to the surface.

**3**

Touch the top of the "J" with the tube, squeeze the bag and pull away from the surface.

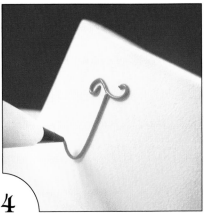

**4**

Curve the bottom of the "J" upwards by closing in to the cake's surface and stop piping.

**5**

Touch the surface with the tube, squeeze the bag and pull away to start the "M".

**6**

Stop piping and close in to the cake's surface, then pull away.

**7**

Continue piping the "M" middle sections, as shown. Start to pipe the last stem.

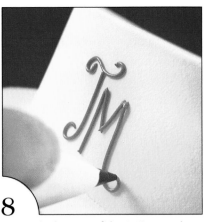

**8**

Curve the bottom of the "M" upwards by closing in to the cake's surface and stop piping.

**9**

Picture shows the completed initials.

Before piping a monogram onto a cake-top or cake-side, draw the chosen initials on a sheet of paper using two colours, one for each initial. By breaking the flow of a line in each initial, an under-and-over effect will be created.

The monogram style can be varied by elongating the initials (as in the "ST") or by reducing the size of one of the initials (as in the "RC").

# PIPING DIRECTIONS FOR
# THE ALPHABET

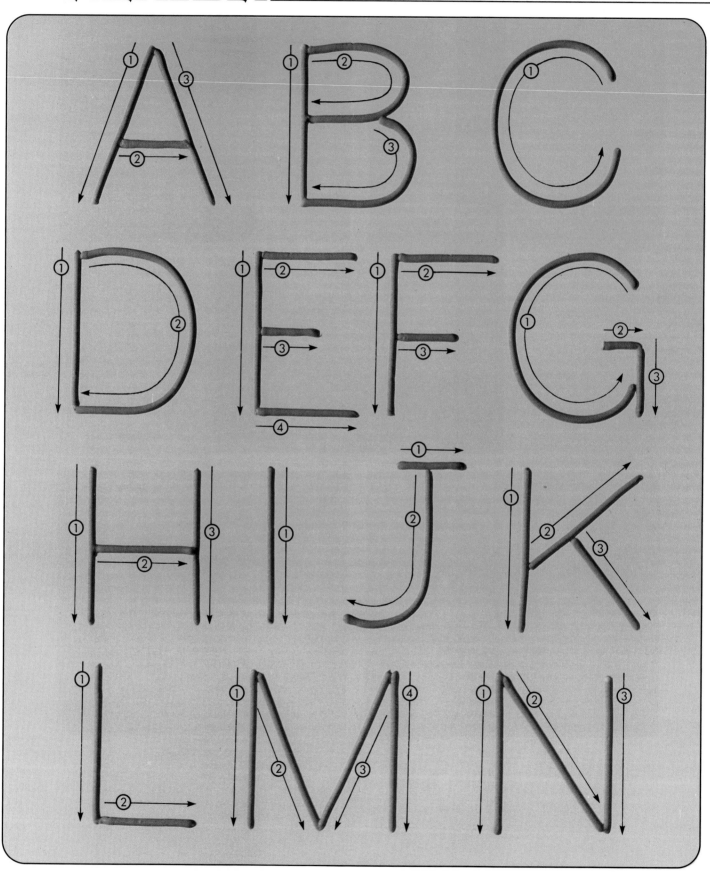

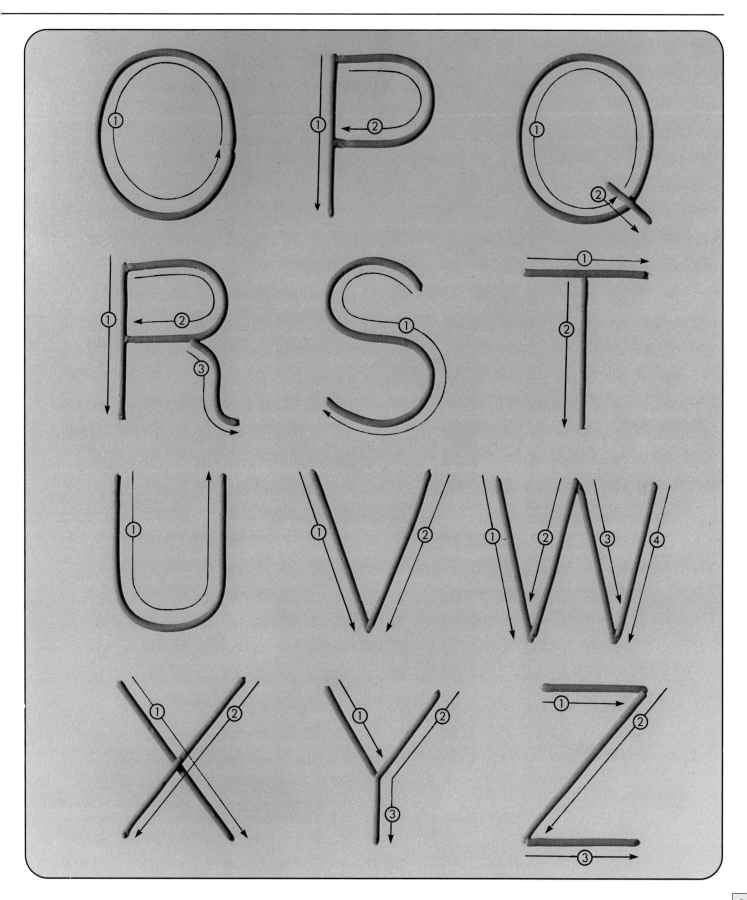

# BASIC PIPED SHAPES

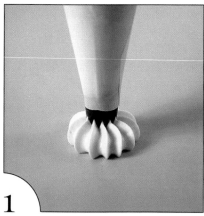

**1**

**Star:** Hold the piping bag still in an upright position and press.

**2**

When the star is the required size, stop pressing and lift the piping bag upright to complete the shape.

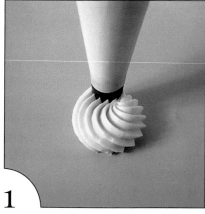

**1**

**Rosette:** Holding the piping bag upright, move and press in a clockwise direction.

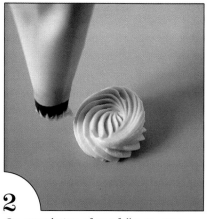

**2**

On completion of one full turn, stop pressing and draw the piping bag away to complete the shape.

**1**

**'C' line:** Holding the piping bag at a slight angle, move and press in an anti-clockwise direction.

**2**

Release the pressure whilst sliding the piping tube along the surface, to form a tail and complete the shape.

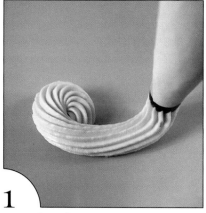

**1**

**Lateral 'C' line:** Pipe in an anti-clockwise direction at an even height to form the first curve.

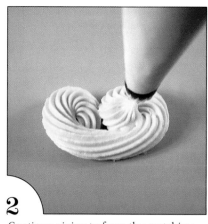

**2**

Continue piping to form the matching curve. Stop piping and lift bag away upright.

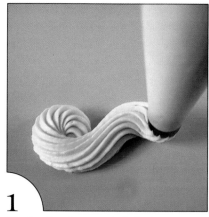

**1**

**Skein:** Pipe in an anti-clockwise direction at an even height to form the first curve.

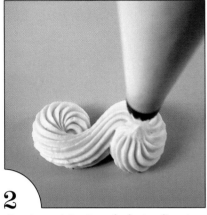

**2**

Continue piping in a clockwise direction to form a matching curve. Stop piping and lift bag upright.

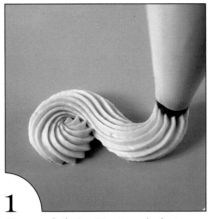

**1**

**Reversed skein:** Pipe in a clockwise direction at an even height to form the first curve.

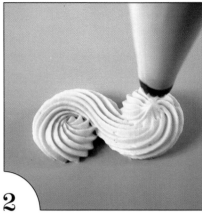

**2**

Continue piping in an anti-clockwise direction and stop when the matching opposite curve is complete, then lift the bag away upright.

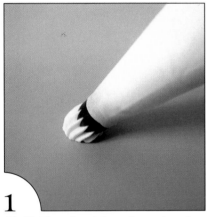

**1**

**Shell:** Place the piping tube against the surface at the angle shown and start to press.

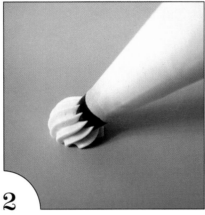

**2**

Continue pressing and start to lift the piping bag.

**3**

With the piping bag slowly moving upwards, continue pressing until the size required is reached.

**4**

Stop pressing, move the piping bag down to the surface and pull away to complete the shape.

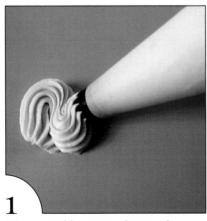

**1**

**Zigzag:** Holding piping bag at a low angle, pipe up and down in an even zigzag along the surface.

**2**

Continue to length required, stop piping and pull away to complete the shape.

**1**

**Rope:** Holding the piping bag at a low angle, pipe a spring shape along the surface in a clockwise direction.

**2**

Continue piping until length required, then stop. Pull the piping bag away to complete the shape.

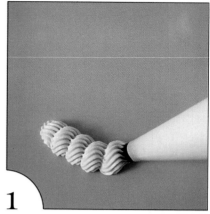

**1**

**Convex rope:** Pipe a spring-shape in a clockwise direction, using even pressure and keeping the bag horizontal.

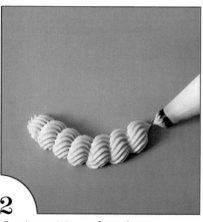

**2**

Continue piping to form the curve shown. Stop piping and pull the bag away in a half-turn.

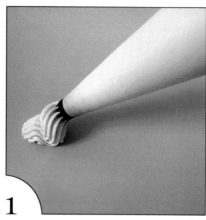

**1**

**Spiral shell:** Hold the piping bag at the angle shown and start to press.

**2**

Continue piping in a clockwise direction, increasing the size of the circle with each turn.

**3**

Continue piping in clockwise direction but, from the centre, decrease the size of the circle with each turn.

**4**

To complete the spiral shell, stop piping and pull bag away in a half-turn.

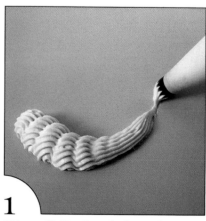

**1**

**'C' scroll:** Pipe in a clockwise direction, increasing size. Continue piping, reducing size then form the tail using reduced pressure.

**1**

**Reversed 'C' Scroll:** Pipe in a clockwise direction, increasing size. Continue piping, reducing the size, then form tail using reduced pressure.

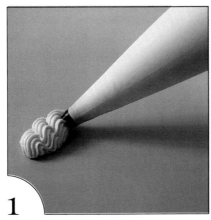

**1**

**'S' Scroll:** Hold piping bag at angle shown and start to press.

**2**

Continue piping in a clockwise direction, increasing the size of each circle to form the body.

**3**

Continue piping, reducing the size of the circles from the centre.

**4**

Continue piping and form the tail by reducing the pressure.

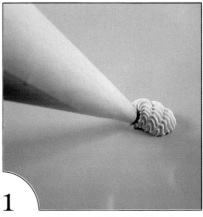

**1**

**Reversed 'S' scroll:** Hold piping bag at angle shown and start to press.

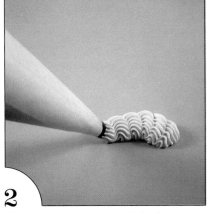

**2**

Continue piping in an anti-clockwise direction, increasing the size of each circle to form the body.

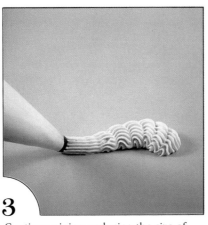

**3**

Continue piping, reducing the size of the circles from the centre.

**4**

Continue piping and form the tail by reducing the pressure.

# PIPING SUGAR FLOWERS AND LEAVES

## PRACTICAL HINTS

Always use freshly made royal icing without glycerin when piping flowers or leaves. This produces sharp edges on flowers and enables the veins on leaves to be clearly seen when dry.

Colour the icing with edible food colouring to match or contrast the colours used on the cake. If using liquid, compensate with additional icing sugar to keep the icing stiff.

Royal icing piped flowers or leaves will keep indefinitely and can be stored in cardboard boxes in a dry atmosphere until required.

The advantage of piped flowers over that of wired is that they make a cake safer to eat, especially when children are involved. Flower nails can be purchased from specialist cake decorating suppliers.

The technique for piping royal icing flowers, described below, can be used to pipe buttercream flowers. The flowers should however be placed in the refrigerator to harden.

Granulated sugar can be coloured by thoroughly mixing in a few drops of food colouring (use a small bowl). Leave to dry 1 hour. Store in a covered container.

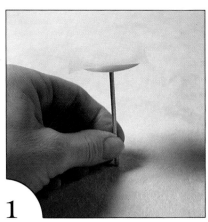

**1**

**Piping a flower:** Cut and fix a piece of waxed paper to the top of a flower nail using royal icing. Hold the nail between finger and thumb in the position shown.

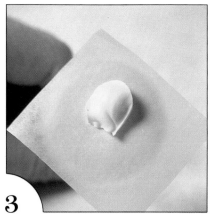

**2**

Hold the piping bag, with tube (No.58), touching the waxed paper as near to horizontal as possible. Ensure the thickest side of the tube is at the centre.

**3**

Pipe a wide petal (to the size required) keeping the bag horizontal whilst pressing, turning the nail as the petal is being piped.

**4**

Pipe a second petal in the same manner as step 2, next to the first petal joining at the side as shown. Ensure that the petals are of even thickness and size.

**5**

Pipe a third and fourth petal using steady pressure on the piping bag to achieve petals of consistent size.

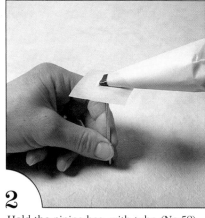

**6**

Pipe the fifth and final petal to complete a uniform shape. Then pipe a bulb in the flower's centre (No.2). Leave to dry for 24 hours.

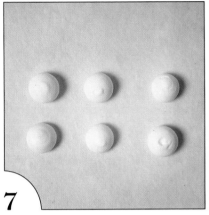

**7**

**Making flower centres:** Pipe bulbs of royal icing onto waxed paper (No.3).

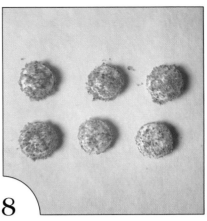

**8**

Immediately sprinkle coloured granulated sugar over the bulbs covering with an even thickness. Leave to dry for 24 hours.

**9**

Remove the sugar coated bulbs and fix to piped flowers, using royal icing.

**10**

A piped flower can be finished with a centre cut from sugarpaste.

**11**

Circles can be piped to form a trumpet, with piped dots in the centre.

**12**

Dots can be piped on the flower's centre to imitate stamens.

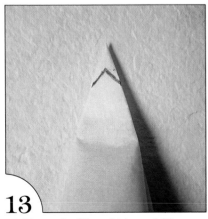

**13**

**Making a leaf bag:** Make and fill a paper piping bag (see p.29) without a piping tube. Mark the tip as shown.

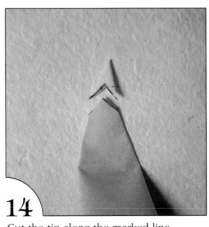

**14**

Cut the tip along the marked line, ensuring both edges are cut to the same angle.

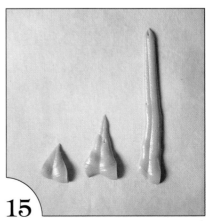

**15**

Pipe leaves in various sizes. The width of the leaf can be altered by cutting the tip to size required.

# TEMPLATES

TEMPLATES

# MAKING A RUNOUT

**1**
Make royal icing without glycerin (see p.17). Cover with a damp cloth for 24 hours. Place small quantity in a bowl and mix in edible food colouring.

**2**
Divide between two bowls. Add, and slowly fold in to one bowl only, cold water a little at a time.

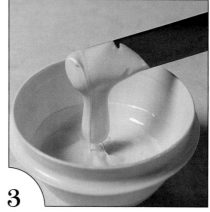

**3**
Continue adding water until a dropping consistency is reached. Cover the bowl with a damp cloth.

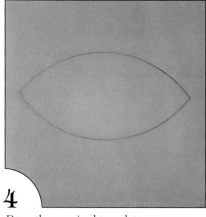

**4**
Draw the required template on paper and then secure it on a tile or flat surface. Overlay the template with a piece of waxed paper and secure.

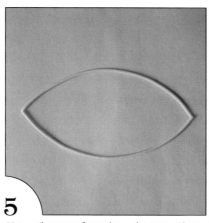

**5**
Using the unsoftened royal icing without glycerin, pipe outline of template (No.2).

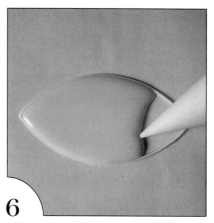

**6**
Fill inside the piped line with the softened royal icing, using a piping bag without a tube. Leave to dry for 24 hours at 18°C (65°F).

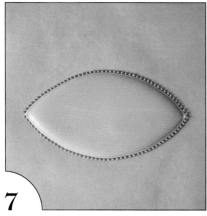

**7**
Using unsoftened royal icing without glycerin, pipe dots around the edge of the runout (No.1)

**8**
Decorate the runout with inscription of choice and piped flowers (No.1). Leave to dry for 24 hours.

**9**
Carefully pull the waxed paper over a table edge to release the runout. Note: Place a cloth under the runout in case it falls.

# MAKING ROSES

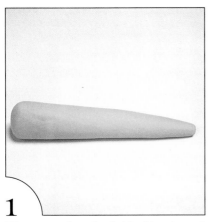

**1**

**How to make a bud:** Mould a piece of flower paste into a long roll, which tapers off one side, as shown.

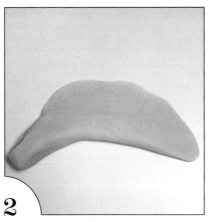

**2**

Flatten and spread one side of the roll to produce a sharp edge.

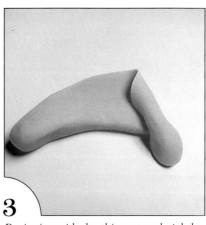

**3**

Beginning with the thinnest end, tightly roll the paste from right to left.

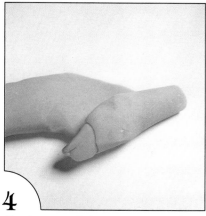

**4**

Continue to roll the paste, turning the base across the main lie of the roll.

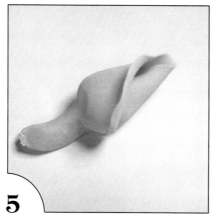

**5**

Cut unwanted paste from base. Shape end of bud between finger and thumb. Curl back and open outer side of petal to complete the bud shape. Leave to dry for 24 hours.

**6**

**How to make a rose:** Repeat steps 1-5. Then cut and remove unwanted paste from the base. Flatten the base and place the bud in an upright position as shown.

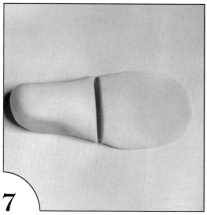

**7**

Roll out a piece of paste, flatten one end to form a thin petal. Cut the petal off as shown.

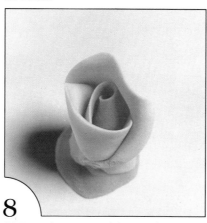

**8**

Moisten the centre of the petal with egg white or cooled boiled water, and wrap it around the upright bud. Repeat steps 7-8 until the shape shown is achieved.

**9**

Continue to make and fix further petals, gently curving each one outwards as it is fixed in position.

**10**

Allow to dry as necessary to avoid the petals collapsing, and continue to add further petals, gradually increasing petal size, until the rose is complete.

**11**

Brush confectioners' dusting powder over the edge of each petal to the strength of colour required for the rose.

**12**

Make and fix a paste calyx and base to the rosebud and colour as desired.

# MAKING SUGAR FLOWERS

**1**

**Making a carnation:** Cut a scalloped disc of sugarpaste or flower paste. Flute the edges by rolling a cocktail stick gently backwards and forwards.

**2**

Immediately fold the disc in half, then gather the edges to form the centre of the flower. Make and add more fluted discs as required.

**3**

When the desired size is achieved, leave until dry. Then colour the carnations with edible food colours or tints.

**1**

**Making blossoms:** Cut sugarpaste or flower paste blossom and place on soft sponge. Indent each petal with a modelling tool. Carefully upturn blossom and indent centre.

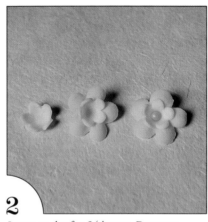

**2**

Leave to dry for 24 hours. Decorate centre as shown using royal icing (No.1) and smaller blossoms.

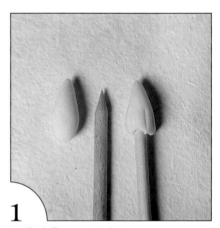

**1**

**Pulled flowers:** Roll a sugarpaste cone and push it on to a pencil shaped stick. Cut six slits in the cone, as indicated.

**2**

Remove sugarpaste and, with finger and thumb, press out each section to a petal shape. Leave to dry for 24 hours. Shade inside the flower with edible food colouring.

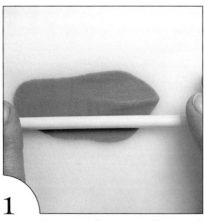

**1**

**Wiring leaves:** Roll out a small piece of sugarpaste or flower paste into a long cone. Roll the top half of the cone thinly, leaving the base thicker.

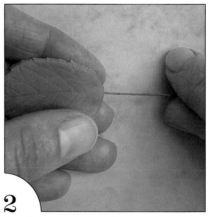

**2**

Carefully cut the leaf shape with thicker portion at base. Smooth edges. Vein with a cocktail stick. Moisten wire with egg white and insert into base.

# GARRETT FRILLS

**1** Lightly dust the work surface with a little cornflour and roll out sugarpaste. Cut the shape shown.

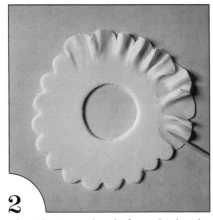

**2** Place the tapered end of a cocktail stick over the edge of the circle and rock it back and forth to create a frill.

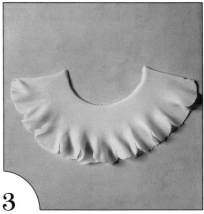

**3** Cut the frilled circle in half. Moisten with a little water and fix to the cake, as required.

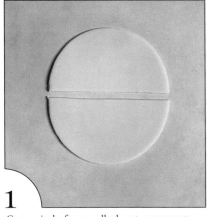

**1** Cut a circle from rolled out sugarpaste and cut in half, as shown.

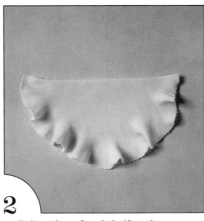

**2** Frill the edge of each half circle as shown in step 2 above.

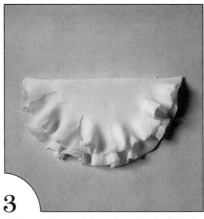

**3** Moisten the straight edge of a half circle and fix one on top of the other.

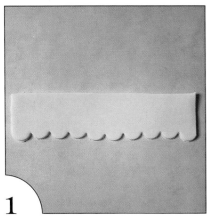

**1** Cut the shape shown from rolled out sugarpaste.

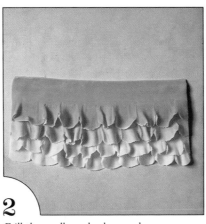

**2** Frill the scalloped edge as shown. Repeat as required. Moisten the straight edges and fix the layers, as shown.

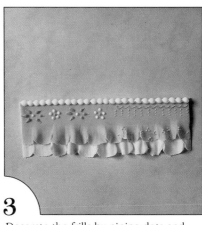

**3** Decorate the frills by piping dots and small shells, as shown, using royal icing.

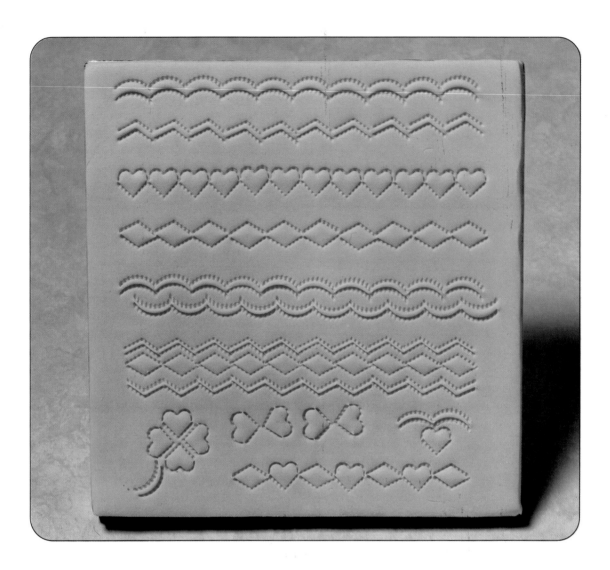

**1**

A crimping tool of appropriate shape is required. Place a rubber band around the tool to bring the teeth 6mm (¼") apart.

**2**

Dip the teeth into sieved icing sugar and tap off the surplus.

**3**

Push the teeth into newly rolled sugarpaste, squeeze together then gently release and raise the crimper. Repeat at even thickness the shape required.

# BRUSHED EMBROIDERY

This delicate technique, which is extremely simple to use, produces a delightful lacy finish that can be coloured to give soft or dramatic effects. Brushed embroidery is a versatile medium that can be used on sugarpaste or royal icing.

Brushed embroidery is particularly suitable for reproducing flowers or lace and is, therefore, an ideal technique for wedding or anniversary cakes. The design should be traced from the template and transferred to the cake-top as shown in step 1 overleaf.

Always use freshly made icing to the recipe given. The piping gel will reduce crusting and the icing will remain workable for longer. The icing can be coloured before use, or painted with edible food colouring or confectioners' dusting powder when dry. If using several colours of icing, an appropriate number of piping bags and tubes will be required. Always work from the outside of the design towards the centre, concentrating on a small area at a time.

The outer line should be piped with a fine writing tube (No.1). The icing is then immediately stroked towards the centre with a fine, damp (but not wet) paintbrush. The brush should be held at 40° angle and used with a long, smooth stroke to draw the icing towards the centre. Leaf veins can be piped on with a fine tube or brushed out with a damp paintbrush.

With thoughtful colouring, the 'flat' appearance can be transformed. For instance, highlighting the same side of leaves and petals will create the effect of light falling at an angle. Using a darker colour for the outer line and a slightly paler one for an inner line produces a subtle play of light and can look very dramatic against a white cake.

A realistic finish can be achieved by carefully reproducing the natural texture and colouring of flowers. Deepening the colour at the base of a petal for example, or darkening the veins on a leaf. Texture and variety can be introduced, particularly if several harmonising colours are woven into the design.

When working brushed embroidery, always remember that coloured icing will be almost impossible to remove completely, so great care should be taken to avoid mistakes in positioning or colour.

## RECIPE
3 tablespoons of royal icing mixed with $1/4$ teaspoon of clear piping gel.

**1**

Draw and cut out paper templates. Place on coated cake-top and scratch template outlines carefully into the coating. Remove the templates.

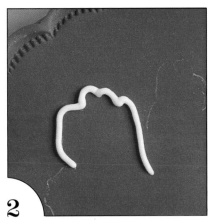

**2**

Pipe a line (No.1) of royal icing mixed with clear piping gel (see p.53) over part of the scratched petal line.

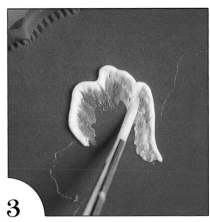

**3**

Immediately brush the icing to the centre of the petal to achieve the effect shown.

## 4

Continue to work one petal at a time until the flower is complete. Then repeat the process for the remaining flower heads.

## 5

Repeat steps 2-4 to complete each leaf, as shown.

## 6

Pipe the stems and flower centres as shown in the main picture.

TEMPLATE

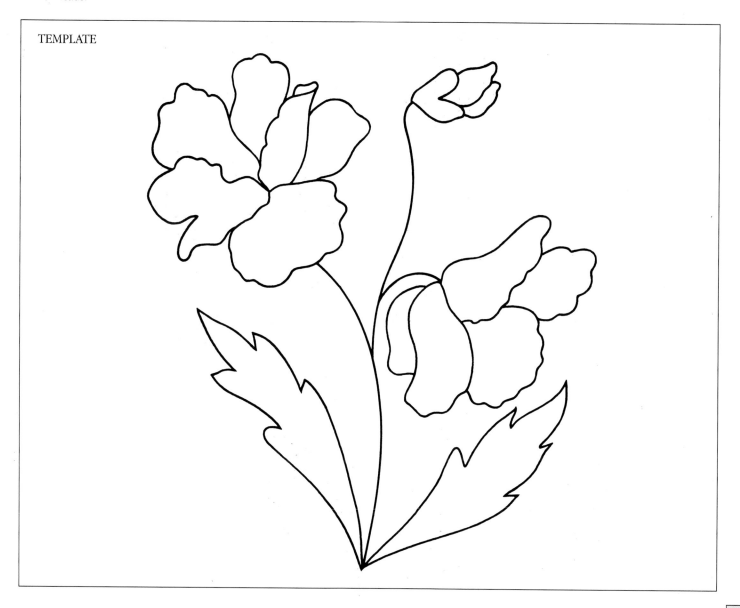

(a)

(c)

(d)

(e)

(f)

(b)

(h)

(g)

(k)      (l)      (m)      (n)      (o)      (p)

(i)

(j)

(q)

# CRYSTALLISING THROUGH THE SEASONS

**SPRING**
Almond Blossom
Apple Blossom
Chamomile
Cherry Blossom
Daisy (m)
Heartsease
Honeysuckle (d)
Japonica
Lemon Balm
Marjoram (q)
Mint (e)
Pansy
Parsley (a)
Pear Blossom
Polyanthus
Primula
Primrose
Sage (g)
Violet

Hibiscus
Honeysuckle (d)
Hyssop
Jasmine
Lavender (b)
Lime Blossom
Marigold (h)
Mimosa
Nasturtium (k)
Passionflower (r)
Pink (l)
Rose (p)
Rosemary (c)
Scented leaf Pelagonium

**AUTUMN**
Clove Pink
Nasturtium (k)
Pansy (f)
Single Chrysanthemum

**SUMMER**
Borage
Carnation (i)
Chive (o)
Cornflower (j)
Dandelion (n)
Evening Primrose

**WINTER**
Jasmine
Freesia

Flowers pictured are
shown in ( ).

57

Crystallised flowers are traditional decorations which are extremely easy to make and most attractive in appearance.

Flowers should be carefully selected to ensure that they are edible. Flowers from a bulb, such as daffodils, snowdrops or lily-of-the-valley, should never be used. The beautiful blue borage flower has a wonderful colour and taste, as do rose petals, violets and nasturtiums. Most fruit-tree blossoms and some shrubs, such as mimosa or japonica, are also suitable for crystallising.

A fine selection of edible flowers and leaves are illustrated on page 56. Flowers should be picked when they have just opened, preferably mid-day when they are completely dry and free from insects. Ensure that the chosen flowers have not been sprayed with insecticide. Discard any which are not perfectly formed or which are shrivelled or blemished.

Flowers crystallised by the method shown below should be used within a few days. However, if required, crystallised flowers can be prepared when the blossom is in season by dissolving one teaspoon of gum arabic in 25ml (1fl.oz.) of water or clear alcohol such as vodka. Paint each petal with the mixture and then proceed from step 4. Dry on a rack in a warm room. Flowers crystallised in this way will keep for several months if stored between layers of tissue paper in an airtight tin.

The finished flowers can make an attractive winter decoration for cakes as well as place or table settings, at a time when fresh flowers are difficult to find. However, the flowers will only keep if they are completely covered in sugar. Crystallised flowers are brittle and should be handled with care, and extra flowers crystallised in case of breakage.

**1**
Carefully select suitable, edible flowers. They should be crystallised within 1 hour of picking. Ensure that flowers have not been sprayed with insecticide.

**2**
Thoroughly mix 2 teaspoons of cold water with 1 fresh egg white in a clean, grease free bowl.

**3**
Using a soft, medium-sized paintbrush, gently cover the top of the flower petals with the egg white and water solution.

**4**

Sprinkle the flowers with caster sugar and gently shake off excess. (Note: sugar can be coloured with confectioners' dusting powder or food colouring.)

**5**

Using the brush, coat the back of the petals, calyx and stem with solution. Sprinkle with sugar. Place on greaseproof paper on a wire tray for 24 hours.

**6**

Leaves can be also crystallised using steps 1-5. Large flowers and roses should be wired around the stem and dried upside down to avoid distortion.

# HINTS AND TIPS

## Baking

It is most important to weigh all ingredients carefully, particularly when using an all-in-one recipe.

Never use eggs out of the refrigerator. Allow to reach room temperature.

All ingredients should preferably be at room temperature.

Make sure all fruit is as dry as possible. Do not overwash the fruit.

Overbeaten batter will not support the fruit, which will sink during baking.

It is important to line the inside of the cake tin carefully to prevent a mis-shape.

Placing a pan of water in the oven creates steam which keeps the cake-top level and moist on top with no crust.

Always use the correct size cake tin for the amount of batter.

Cakes should be baked on the centre shelf of the oven unless specified.

Cover fruit cakes with greaseproof paper if the top starts to colour too much.

Never bake a cake in a brand new, shiny, tin. The shine can be removed by placing the empty tin in a hot oven.

Ensure that the oven is at the correct temperature for the recipe, and test as directed after the recommended time.

Allow three weeks for a fruit cake to mature.

## Almond paste

Always ensure that all equipment is scrupulously clean.

Do not overmix almond paste.

Use only the best quality ground almonds.

Never allow flour to come into contact with almond paste.

Almond paste can be gently warmed in the oven until pliable.

## Covering a cake in almond paste

Ensure that the cake is as level as possible.

Roll out almond paste on icing or caster sugar.

Only use apricot purée for brushing as this has the least colour and flavour.

## Buttercream

To obtain best result, always use fresh butter at a temperature of 18-21°C (65-70°F)

Coloured or toasted dessicated coconut, vermicelli or biscuit crumbs can be used as decoration.

## Piping

Practice piping on an upturned cake tin.

Always pipe onto a dry surface.

Always make up sufficient coloured icing as it is almost impossible to match colours at a later stage.

Leave used tubes overnight in cold water.

## Sugarpaste

Sugarpaste should be made 24 hours before use.

If the paste is too dry, add a little white fat or egg white.

If the paste is too sticky, add a little cornflour or icing sugar.

In cold weather, warm the paste slightly in the oven.

If a crust has formed, remove before use.

# What went wrong with the cake?

| | | |
|---|---|---|
| Cracked crusted top | – | Too hot an oven or baked too high in oven |
| Domed top | | |
| Uncooked centre | | |
| Dark in colour | | |
| Burnt fruit or top | | |
| | | |
| Pale cake | – | Too cool an oven |
| Uncooked fruit | | |
| Very thick crust | | |
| | | |
| Hollow top | – | Overbeating. Insufficient or too slow cooking time. Oven door slammed. Tin too small |
| | | |
| Close 'damp' texture | – | Too slow cooking. Not baked long enough |
| | | |
| Coarse texture | – | Inadequate mixing. Oven too cool |
| | | |
| Rubbery texture | – | Over-mixing. Too much egg |
| | | |
| Crumbly texture | – | Inadequate mixing. Overbeating. Cooked too slowly. Insufficient sugar |
| | | |
| Uneven texture | – | Inadequate mixing |
| | | |
| Air pockets | – | Mixture too dry. Mixture not all poured into tin at one time |
| | | |
| Fruit sinks | – | Overbeaten batter. Mixture too wet |

| | | |
|---|---|---|
| Crusty sides | – | Over-greased tin |
| | | |
| Cake top speckled | – | Too much sugar. Sugar too coarse |
| | | |
| Cake sticks to tin | – | Tin inadequately greased or lined |
| | | |
| Cake goes stale | – | Incorrect storage. Mixture too dry |
| | | |
| Icing stained | – | Almond paste too thin |
| | | |
| Almond paste ferments | – | Flour or cornflour used for rolling out. Apricot purée not boiled |
| | | |
| Almond paste oily | – | Overmixed |
| | | |
| Butter cream has bitter taste | – | Food colour too strong |
| | | |
| Royal icing is not smooth | – | Insufficiently mixed. Too much icing sugar added |
| | | |
| Icing is patchy | – | Uneven coating |
| | | |
| Icing is too hard | – | Insufficient beating. Too much icing sugar added. No glycerin |
| | | |
| Runout seeps | – | Inadequate outline. Icing too soft |

# DECORATIVE CAKE-TOPS

**1**

Using different shaped crimpers, press into sugarpaste (before drying) to form the border. Decorate as required.

**2**

Coat cake-top with buttercream or royal icing and immediately pattern half, using a comb scraper. Pipe skeins (No.7) and decorate (see p.41).

**3**

Pipe shells around an oval cake (No.7). Then pipe a leaf between each shell, using a leaf bag (see p.45). Decorate with large flowers and graduated dots (No.1).

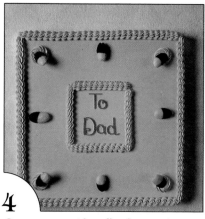

**4**

Coat sponge with coffee flavoured buttercream. Pipe a continuous rope line around the edge and in centre (No.6). Decorate with almonds dipped in chocolate.

**5**

Using a template, cut and fix a sugarpaste number on a chocolate buttercream covered sponge. Pipe spiral shells and plain shells, as shown (No.7).

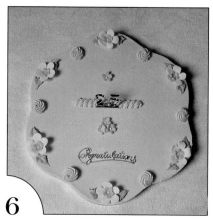

**6**

Cover petal shaped cake with sugarpaste and decorate with piped rosettes (No.7). Make and fix sugarpaste flowers (see p.50), then pipe the leaves using a leaf bag.

**7**

Place coated cake on a turntable and rotate, using a comb scraper to create rings. Make and fix sugarpaste frilled plaque (see p.51) with sugarpaste leaves and berries around edge.

**8**

Cover a buttercream coated sponge with a triangle of sugarpaste. Crimp around edge of sugarpaste and then pipe stars (No.13) along remaining sides. Top with silver dragee.

**9**

Pipe edge of buttercream coated sponge with 'C' lines (No.7). Decorate with lemon slices, jelly diamonds and a sugarpaste or artifical rose (see p.48).

**10**
Decorate cake edge with scrolls and shells (No.43). Pipe line (No.2). Pipe stork's body and initial letters (No.2). Pipe beak, legs and remaining letters (No.1).

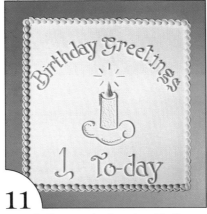

**11**
Pipe shells around cake-edge (No.3) and over-pipe (No.2). Pipe Birthday Greetings and 1 To-day (No.2). Overpipe (No.1), then pipe the candle to fit remaining space (No.1).

**12**
Pipe scalloped line around cake-top edge (No.1). Pipe name (No.2), then message (No.1). Fix a sugarpaste sun and decorate with piped lines (No.2).

**13**
Pipe shells around the cake-top edge (No.44). Then pipe the numeral (No.3) and the remaining letters (No.2) to fit, using card guides where necessary (see p.30).

**14**
Using straight lines pipe the message with alternate colours (No.1). Decorate with sugarpaste cut-out shapes. Pipe a rosette in each corner (No.43) and shells (No.43).

**15**
Divide the cake-top into portions with a piped line (No.2). Then pipe the centre message and musical notes, followed by a name in each section (No.1). Decorate with a guitar.

**16**
Use a guide to position lettering on cake-top (see p.30) and pipe message (No.1). Decorate with tracery (No.1). Pipe shells around edge (No.43) and fix candles.

**17**
Pipe 'C' scrolls around cake-top edge (No.44). Make and fix floral spray then, using strips of card as guide lines, pipe the message (No.2). Pipe scrolled line (No.2).

**18**
Cut template for box and pipe outline (No.2). Remove template when dry. Filigree centre (No.1), then complete piping (No.2). Pipe shells and 'S' and 'C' scrolls (No.42).

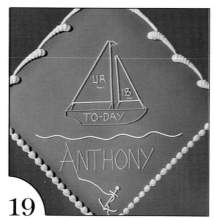

**19**

Pipe boat outline (No.1) and remove template when dry. Then pipe name, waves, anchor and rope (Nos.2 & 1). Pipe 'C' scrolls and shells (No.43) as shown.

**20**

Pipe the message in a flowing style (No.2). Then decorate with tracery (No.1). Complete with a key. Pipe shells around cake-top edge (No.44).

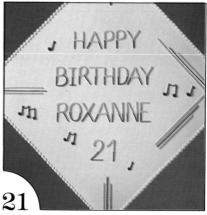

**21**

Pipe message, corner lines and music (No.2). Overpipe the bottom half of letters in contrasting colour, as shown (No.1). Pipe lines (Nos.2 & 1) and shells (No.3).

**22**

Make and fix the floral spray with royal icing. Then pipe the message (No.2). Decorate spray with graduated dots (No.1). Pipe large 'C' scrolls around edge (No.44).

**23**

Pipe the upright lines, then remaining lines to complete the words (No.2). Decorate as shown (No.1). Pipe edge with 'S' and 'C' scrolls (No.43) and piped line (No.2).

**24**

Pipe all the straight lines first, using strips of card as guide (No.2). Then pipe message (No.2), overpipe (No.1), and enhance with scalloped lines and flowers.

**25**

Make run-out initials (see p.47). Pipe dividing lines (Nos.2 & 1). Fix initials and spray. Pipe bottom edge with shells (No.2), top edge with scallops and dots (No.1).

**26**

Pipe message using guide strips (No.1). Pipe, and overpipe, square corners using template (Nos.2 & 1). Pipe scallops and dots (No.1). Pipe spirals. Decorate with flowers.

**27**

Using guide strips, pipe, and overpipe, message in different colour icings (Nos.2 & 1). Pipe shells around cake-top edge (no.7). Decorate with cricketers.

**28**

Pipe the message (No.1). Then decorate with tracery. Pipe shells around cake-top edge (No.44). Position and fix, with royal icing, a heart and a rose.

**29**

Using guide lines, pipe message (No.2). Overpipe (No.1). Underline with tracery and dots (No.1). Decorate cake-top edge with scrolls as shown (No.43).

**30**

Using guide strips pipe congratulations first and then names (No.2). Overpipe (No.1). Underline with tracery (No.1). Pipe 'S' scrolls (No.44) and piped line (No.3).

**31**

Outline and flood-in a large heart (see p.47). Leave to dry for 24 hours. Fix heart and pipe wording as shown (Nos.2 & 1). Pipe bows and dots (No.1), scrolls and shells (No.43).

**32**

Pipe, and overpipe, congratulations (Nos.2 & 1). Then pipe the names and tracery (No.1). Pipe 'S' and 'C' scrolls on cake-top corners and shells around edges (No.43).

**33**

Using guide strips, pipe the initial letters (No.1). Overpipe bottom half with small rope (No.1). Pipe tracery. Pipe shells around edge (No.43). Fix flower spray.

**34**

Make and fix a sugarpaste banner. Decorate with small plane and pipe message, linking the decoration with flowing lines (No.1). Pipe shells around edge (No.43).

**35**

Using template as guide, pipe flag (No.2). Remove when dry. Pipe flag pole (No.3), then message (Nos.2 & 1). Decorate edge with 'S' and 'C' scrolls (No.43) and piped line (No.2).

**36**

Pipe the flower motif (Nos.2 & 1). Leave to dry. Then pipe, and overpipe, message and monogram (Nos.3 & 2). Pipe shells around cake-top edge (No.42).

**37**

Using a template as guide, pipe heart shape with shells (No.2). Then pipe, and overpipe, the message and decorate (Nos.2 & 1). Pipe shells around cake-top edge (No.43).

**38**

Pipe the straight initial line first (No.2) then overpipe (No.1). Pipe remaining letters and decorative lines (Nos.2 & 1). Pipe shells around the cake-top edge (No.43).

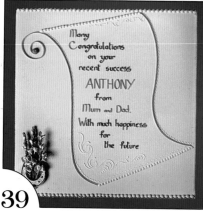

**39**

Pipe scroll outline (Nos.2 & 1). Pipe shells on scroll-top edge (No.2). Pipe scalloped line, message and tracery (No.1). Pipe, and overpipe, shells (Nos.3 & 2).

**40**

Using a template, pipe horseshoe outline (No.2). Remove template when dry. Pipe name and motif (No.2). Pipe 'S' and 'C' scrolls around the cake-top edge (No.43).

**41**

Make and fix a plaque (see p.47). Decorate edge (No.1). Fix flowers then pipe stems and leaves (see p.45). Pipe message (No.2) and dots, then underline (No.1). Pipe edge as shown.

**42**

Make runout letter (see p.47). Pipe flower motif (No.1). When dry, fix letter on top. Pipe pattern around motif (Nos.2 & 1). Complete message (Nos.2 &1). Pipe shells (No.43).

**43**

Using guide strips, pipe message (Nos.2 & 1). Overpipe initial letters in darker colour. Pipe tracery (No.1). Pipe 'C' scrolls (No.42). Fix decorations as shown.

**44**

Using guide strips, pipe white letters (No.2). Overpipe in contrasting shells. (Nos.2 & 1). Pipe tracery. Pipe 'C' scrolls and overpipe (No.3). Fix decorations.

**45**

Make letters and numbers (see p.47). When dry, fix with royal icing. Add flowers and bells and decorate. Pipe a scalloped rope around cake-top edge (No.44).

**46**

Using guide strips, pipe message (No.2). Decorate as shown (No.1). Pipe rabbits (No.2). Add piped flowers (see p.44). Pipe 'C' scrolls around cake-top edge (No.44).

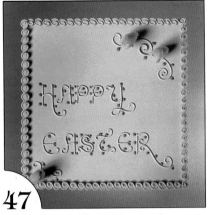

**47**

Pipe message (No.2). Pipe the dots (No.1). Pipe scrolls and dots to match (Nos.2 & 1). Fix chickens. Pipe shells and overpipe with an 'S' line (No.2).

**48**

Pipe Halloween (No.2) and overpipe (No.1). Decorate as shown. Fix sugarpaste stars. Pipe faces (Nos.2 & 1). Pipe shells on two-thirds of cake-edge (No.42).

**49**

Using guide lines and square letters, pipe, and overpipe, message (Nos.2 & 1). Underline as shown (No.1). Pipe 'C' scrolls around the cake-top edge (No.44).

**50**

Using guide lines and curved letters, pipe, and overpipe, the message (Nos.2 & 1). Underline (No.1). Pipe 'C' scrolls around cake-top edge (No.44), and graduated dots (No.1).

**51**

Pipe motif and holly leaves (No.1). Pipe message (No.3). Overpipe (No.2). Fix robin. Pipe scrolls and shells around cake-top edge (No.43).

**52**

Pipe initials (Nos.3 & 1). Pipe remaining letters (No.2). Pipe candles 6mm (¼") tube. Highlight flame (No.2). Pipe 'S' and 'C' scrolls and shells (No.43). Pipe line (No.2).

**53**

Using template as guide, pipe lines to form star (No.1). Remove template when dry. Pipe message and decorate appropriately (No.1). Fix bells and holly with royal icing.

**54**

Make runout letters (see p.47). When dry, brush on royal icing snow. Fix into position. Stipple cake-top with snow. Pipe shells around remainder (No.42).

**55**

Pipe message (No.2), overpipe (No.1). Decorate with lines and bells (No.1). Pipe 'S' scrolls and shells around cake-top edge (No.4). Fix holly and robin.

**56**

Using guide lines, pipe message (No.2), overpipe bottom with shells (No.1). Fix decorations. Pipe decorations. Pipe tracery (No.1). Pipe 'C' scrolls (Nos.43 & 42) and spiral scrolls (No.43).

**57**

Make runout letters (see p.47). Decorate with holly leaves. Position and fix letters. Pipe tracery (No.1). Fix holly and bells. Decorate with 3 short lines (No.1).

**58**

Make sugarpaste book (see p.136), then pipe message and tracery (No.1). Position and fix book. Pipe message underneath and decorate with tracery and dots (No.1).

**59**

Using template, cut and fix a sugarpaste tree. Pipe message down centre (Nos.2 & 1). Pipe names (Nos.2 & 1), bucket (No.2) and then stipple on snow. Pipe edges with shells (No.43).

**60**

Fix Father Christmas to centre. Pipe lines and message (Nos.2 & 1). Make sugar bells and fix to corner (see p.143). Pipe shells around cake-top edge (No.43).

**61**

Using guide lines, pipe, and overpipe, message with initials in different colour (Nos.2 & 1). Pipe tracery (No.1). Pipe 'S' and 'C' scrolls (No.44). Fix robins.

**62**

Using guide lines, pipe message (No.2). Overpipe top half in dots (No.1). Underline as shown (No.1). Pipe scrolls and shells (No.43) and outline (No.2) on edge.

**63**

Make and fix sugarpaste balloons, then pipe lines and message (No.1). Make, decorate and fix plaque (see p.47). Add ribbon bow. Pipe shells around top edge (No.42).

# CHRISTMAS CAKE-TOPS

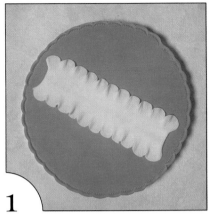

**1**

**Round cake:** Crimp the top edge of a sugarpaste covered cake before it dries. Make and fix a frilled sugarpaste ribbon (see p.51) across the cake-top.

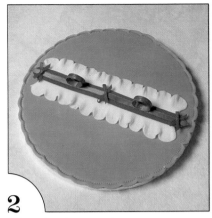

**2**

When dry, decorate the sugarpaste ribbon with food-approved ribbon, loops and bows as shown (using royal icing to fix).

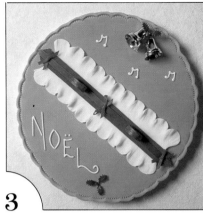

**3**

Using royal icing, pipe message and musical notes (No.1). Fix bells and holly with royal icing to complete the cake.

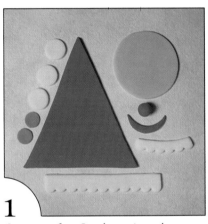

**1**

**Square cake:** Cut the various shapes shown from sugarpaste. Leave to dry for 24 hours.

**2**

When dry, assemble then fix the pieces onto the dry cake-top, using royal icing.

**3**

Stipple some icing with a sponge into the top corners to form snow effect. Pipe shells around the edge (No.7) and dots (No.1). Then pipe message of choice (No.1).

**1**

**Oval cake:** Using a 6mm (¼") diameter piping tube, pipe the two candle sticks. Make and fix sugarpaste flames. Pipe shells down candle side (No.2).

**2**

Make and fix sugarpaste holly leaves and berries, as shown, using royal icing. Fix motto and robin.

**3**

Pipe 'C' scrolls around half the cake edge (No.43), then pipe the shells (No.3). Decorate with piped lines and dots (No.1).

# BUTTERCREAM

Buttercream is an extremely useful coating for sponges and children's birthday cakes as it is versatile and easy to apply. It can be spread quickly and combed to produce an interesting pattern with very little effort, or piped for a more intricate design. Delicate filigree or pretty flowers will add to the appeal. (If artificial flowers are used, these should not be silk as it takes up fat from the buttercream and becomes marked.) A striking design can be produced by crystallising fruit, as shown on page 77, and using this for decoration – although it should be borne in mind that crystallised fruit does not have the keeping properties of crystallised flowers.

Buttercream is the ideal medium for novelty cakes, particularly when combined with sugarpaste decorations, and children love its sweet taste. Young and old alike, however, enjoy the colours and textures that can be created in buttercream. The sides of the cake can be coated with grated chocolate, toasted almonds or combed with a scraper. If the top is to be piped, the buttercream-coated cake should be chilled in a refrigerator for an hour before decorating as this makes the surface firmer to work on.

Colouring, or flavouring, buttercream is a simple process but care should be taken not to use too much as these can be strong and bitter. A few drops should be added at a time until the desired colour or taste is achieved. The taste can be co-ordinated with the colour, lemon flavouring with yellow icing for instance, or mint with green. Coffee or liqueur buttercream is a sophisticated taste for adults whilst both children and adults enjoy the luscious taste of chocolate. If chocolate is to be added to the buttercream, this should be melted first in a bowl over warm water and then added to warmed buttercream. The texture can be varied by adding ingredients such as marshmallow, nuts or whisked egg white.

Chocolate for piping should be prepared as shown on page 74, care being taken not to add too much glycerin as otherwise the chocolate may become too thick. The mixture should be placed in a piping bag whilst still warm and any spare chocolate kept warm in a basin over warm water. Alternatively, nuts can be dipped in chocolate and used to decorate the cake, or chocolate shavings can be sprinkled on the top.

Buttercream is ideal for piping decorative flowers (see page 44). Using two colours of buttercream in the piping bag creates a very attractive flower. The finished flower should be placed in the refrigerator to harden before handling.

## Variations

**Coffee:** using the recipe on page 16, replace 1 tablespoon of water with coffee essence or strong black coffee. Alternatively, replace 2-3 teaspoons of the icing sugar with coffee powder and beat in well.

**Chocolate:** dissolve 1-2 tablespoons of sifted cocoa powder in a little hot water, cool and beat into the icing sugar to replace some of the water. Alternatively, use recipe on page 16, step 6.

**Fruit:** replace the water with fruit juice and beat in well. Add a few drops of food colouring if required.

**Liqueur:** replace the water with brandy, sherry, liqueur of choice, etc.

**Nut:** stir 2 tablespoons of finely chopped walnuts or almonds into the buttercream.

# RITCHIE

**1**

Layer sponge and coat with buttercream. Cover side with nuts, biscuit crumbs or toasted coconut. Using crimped cutter, cut sugarpaste and place on to cake-top centre.

**2**

Fix figure and inscription with buttercream, then decorate with piped dots (No.1). Pipe rosettes around the cake-top edge (No.13).

**3**

Colour dessicated coconut with food colouring and carefully sprinkle in a line around the cake-top. Place a jelly diamond between each rosette to complete the cake.

**1**
Pipe twelve large flowers (see p.44), with buttercream (No.59) onto waxed paper. Leave in refrigerator for 24 hours.

**2**
Fix the flowers around the cake-top as shown with buttercream, then pipe leaves using a leaf bag (see p.45). Fix decoration in centre.

**3**
Fix orange and lemon slices around the cake-base and top, then pipe the leaves shown.

# CHERRY

**1** Layer a sponge with filling then coat with buttercream. Cover the side with roasted chopped nuts. Place a round cutter in the centre of the top.

**2** Sprinkle chopped nuts inside the cutter to make a neat circle. With melted chocolate, pipe swirls around the top, as shown, using a bag without a piping tube.

**3** Pipe rosettes around the edge and inner circle (No.7). Decorate with jelly diamonds and half glacé cherries.

# TEDDIE

**1**

Carefully push coloured coconut around the cake-base to create a band effect on a buttercream coated cake.

**2**

Place 340g (12oz) of chocolate flavoured cake covering in a bowl over a saucepan of water.

**3**

Simmer the water to allow the chocolate to melt slowly. Then mix ¾ teaspoon of glycerin into the chocolate. Keep the mixture warm during use.

74

**4**

Using templates as guide pipe one large bear and twelve small, with the prepared chocolate onto waxed or greaseproof paper.

**5**

When set, pipe-in the feature shown using melted white chocolate. Leave in a cool place until set.

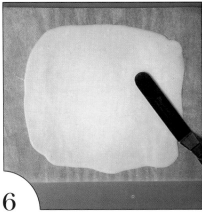

**6**

Spread white chocolate thinly onto waxed or greaseproof paper approximately 10cm (4") square. Leave until just setting.

**7**

Cut out a disc before the chocolate sets completely. Then pipe message of choice (No.1).

**8**

Remove the bears from the waxed paper and fix around the cake-base.

**9**

Fix the large bear onto the cake-top and sprinkle coloured coconut to form the ground.

**10**

Pipe a rosette on each cake-top corner and base (No.6). Then fix split almonds, as shown.

**11**

Pipe the design shown on each cake-top edge (No.6).

**12**

Fix candles and holders with piped rosettes, as required.

TEMPLATES

# GRANDAD

**1**

Brush small bunches of grapes with fresh egg white then cover in caster sugar. Leave to dry for 2 hours.

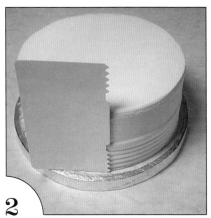

**2**

Using a patterned scraper, coat the sides of an oval sponge cake with buttercream to create the design shown.

**3**

Carefully place the grapes onto the cake-top. Pipe bulbs as shown (No.3). Decorate and fix an appropriate plaque.

**1**

Make the various parts shown, using sugarpaste. Leave until dry. 8 sets required.

**2**

Assemble the parts and decorate with royal icing, as shown (No.1).

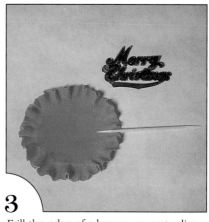

**3**

Frill the edge of a large sugarpaste disc to use in the cake-top centre. Leave until dry.

78

**4**
Cut out sugarpaste holly leaves (see template on p.183) and paint veins, as shown. Leave until dry. 24 required.

**5**
Using a comb shaped scraper, coat the cake-side to form the pattern shown.

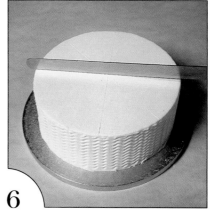

**6**
Mark the top of the cake into eight equal portions.

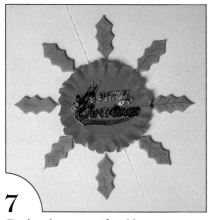

**7**
Fix the plaque, motif and leaves onto the cake-top, pressing gently.

**8**
Pipe a buttercream rope along each marked line (No.7).

**9**
Fix the faces around the cake-top edge, all looking outward.

**10**
Pipe rosettes around the cake-base (No.7).

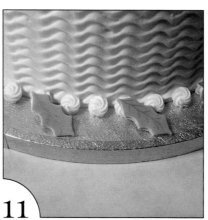

**11**
Fix holly leaves on the rosettes, using two for each section.

**12**
Pipe holly berries on each cake-base leaf (No.1).

# SUGARPASTE

Sugarpaste is an ideal medium for the beginner to work in as its smooth, silky finish requires very little decoration to create a stunning effect. Suitable for celebration cakes of all kinds, it is particularly effective on wedding cakes. Available ready-made if required, it goes on in one operation and provides an instant covering that can be coloured and flavoured easily. It can be rolled and cut out into many shapes or used to create frills, and can be moulded by hand into attractive decorations.

Instructions for covering a cake in sugarpaste are shown on page 24. The smoother the almond paste, the better the sugarpaste finish will be. Brushing a clear alcoholic liquor, such as vodka, bacardi or gin, over the almond paste has a sterilising effect that helps to prevent the formation of mould. Coloured alcohol should not be used as this may discolour the sugarpaste. Alternatively, sponge cakes can be coated in a very thin layer of buttercream, chilled for 1 hour in a refrigerator and then covered in sugarpaste. Fix sugarpaste to sugarpaste with clear alcohol, egg white or cooled, boiled water.

Sugarpaste should be made 24 hours before use and stored in a cool place (not a refrigerator) in an airtight container. Sugarpaste can be made up to two weeks prior to use and stored in a refrigerator, but it must be brought to room temperature before use. Sugarpaste should be rolled out on an icing sugar or cornflour dusted surface. When applying sugarpaste, great care should be taken to avoid trapping air under the paste. If an air bubble does appear, use a pin with a large coloured head to prick it, remove the pin, and then smooth again.
If required, the cake board can also be covered in sugarpaste (no almond paste is required on the cake board). If the cake is to be crimped, this must be done immediately, otherwise the cake should then be left to form a crust. Sugarpaste normally takes 24 hours to dry in a warm room but will take longer in damp and humid weather.

## Colouring and Flavouring Sugarpaste
As liquid may affect the texture, sugarpaste should be coloured with edible paste food colouring. Dip a cocktail stick or skewer into the colour and add a very small amount at a time to the paste. Knead well until the colour is thoroughly mixed. Roll the paste out thinly to check that there is no streaking. Sufficient sugarpaste should always be coloured at one time as it will be virtually impossible to match the colour later. Graduated colours of sugarpaste can be made by adding white sugarpaste to the dark base colour as shown on page 144.

Coloured sugarpaste should be protected from strong light by storing in a sealed container. When the cake has been decorated it should be kept in a cardboard box at a constant temperature of 18°C (65°F).

Sugarpaste is easily flavoured and this can counteract the sweetness of the paste. Always use flavourings sparingly and test the taste before covering the cake. A drop or two of almond essence produces an agreeable flavour but the flavour can be linked to the colour. Oil of peppermint, for instance, is ideal for white or green cakes; whilst raspberry flavouring is appropriate for pinks, and citrus fruits for orange or lemon paste. Vanilla essence should be used for blue cakes.

Sugarpaste can also be dusted or painted once it is dry using confectioners' dusting powder or edible food colourings.

## Modelling Paste
Modelling paste should be used whenever extra strength is required such as in the cut-out figures on page 152 or the collars on page 147. The addition of 2 teaspoons of gum tragacanth to the basic sugarpaste recipe on page 18 will provide sufficient strength for the items in this book. Gum tragacanth can also be kneaded into ready-made sugarpaste in the quantity of 2 teaspoons to 455g (1lb) of sugarpaste. Always ensure

that the gum tragacanth is worked well in. Leave for 24 hours before use. Store as for sugarpaste.

## Crimping

Crimping must be carried out before the sugarpaste has dried as otherwise the paste will crack. A variety of crimper shapes are available although it is possible to improvise with a bottle top for instance. As crimping cannot be removed once completed, it is worth practising using a crimper on a piece of sugarpaste before starting work on the cake. When working, hold the crimper at right angles to the cake and push gently into the paste before squeezing the crimper (see page 52). Release the pressure and then remove.

## Embossing

Embossing, as used on the wedding cake on page 130, must also be carried out on freshly applied sugarpaste. The end of a paintbrush or a teaspoon makes a useful embossing tool.

## Ribbon Work

Food-approved ribbons are a useful way to add colour and impact to a cake, and a carefully placed ribbon can give the finishing touch as can be seen from page 106. The most suitable ribbon is double-sided polyester satin with woven edges as this does not fray. It is available in a wide range of colours and widths. As it holds its shape well, it can be used to create loops and bows.

To attach ribbon to the side of a cake, carefully mark the position by lightly scratching a line around the cake. Place the cake on a turntable (or upturned plate) and then pipe a dot of royal icing onto the cake and fix the ribbon with a large-headed pin. Slowly turn the turntable, positioning the ribbon and fixing as you work. Leave a slight overlap, cut off the spare ribbon and fix into place with royal icing. When the icing is dry, remove the pins.

Ribbon insertion is a pretty technique which is quite simple to carry out. It creates the effect of ribbon woven through the sugarpaste, as can be seen from the cake on page 108. The work should be carried out on sugarpaste which has formed a crust but not dried too hard. The design should be marked on the cake and sufficient pieces of ribbon cut to complete the work. The ribbon should be cut slightly longer than the gap to be filled as the ends need to be tucked well in. A fine blade or long pin should be used to insert the ribbons and no further fixing should be needed.

## Frills

Frills look very attractive on the side of a cake, especially where graduated colours are used, as the light shines through to create a translucent effect. The paste needs to be rolled extremely thinly for maximum effect (see page 51). Frills should be attached to a dry sugarpaste covered cake by lightly moistening with cooled, boiled water. The join can be covered with royal icing.

## Collars

Modelling paste collars, which are simple to make, create an interesting effect on top of a cake. When dry, collars should be attached to the cake with royal icing. They can be further decorated with piping and frills, as shown on page 149.

# BONNIE

**1**

Cover the cake and board with
sugarpaste. Leave to dry for 24 hours.
Fix ribbons as shown.

**2**

Fold a template onto 8 sections (see
p.28). Cut to shape shown and place
onto the cake-top.

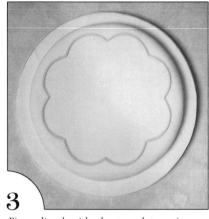

**3**

Pipe a line beside the template, using
royal icing without glycerin (No.3).

**4** Carefully remove the template. Then pipe dots for flowers (No.2).

**5** Pipe inscription of choice on the cake-top (No.2 and 1).

**6** Fix decoration and candle(s). Then pipe small dots for flowers (No.1).

TEMPLATES

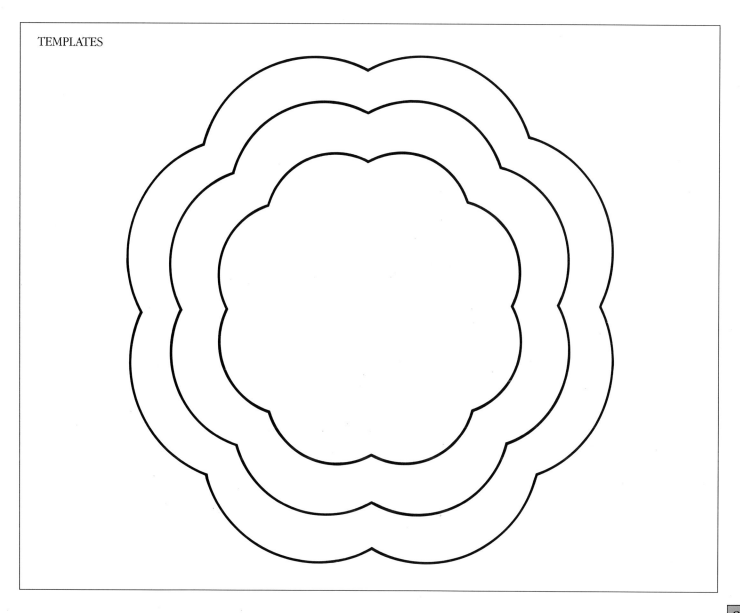

**1**

Cover cake in sugarpaste then immediately crimp the cake-top edge and board. Fix ribbon as shown.

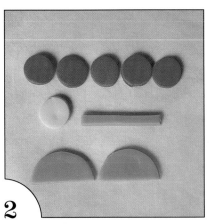

**2**

Roll out and cut sugarpaste pieces to form flowers. Leave to dry for 2 hours.

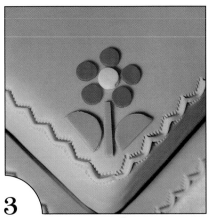

**3**

Assemble, then fix the pieces to each cake-top corner, as shown, using clear alcohol, egg white or cooled, boiled water.

**4** Fix further pieces around the cake-base and sides.

**5** Fix a sugarpaste plaque to the cake-top, then decorate with a purchased cake inscription and sugarpaste pieces as shown.

**6** Make and fix ribbon bows around the cake-top edge. Fix horseshoes onto the cake board.

TEMPLATES

# JUMBO

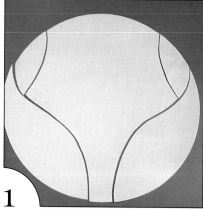

**1** Trace the template onto plain card and cut along the dotted lines to form the various shapes shown. Using the template as a guide, cut a filled sponge into pieces.

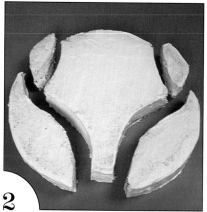

**2** Coat the top and sides of each piece with a thin layer of buttercream. Chill for 1 hour in the refrigerator.

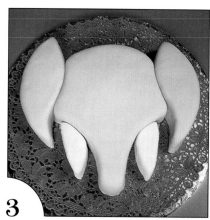

**3** Cover each piece with sugarpaste and then arrange on a doyley covered board to form 'Jumbo'.

86

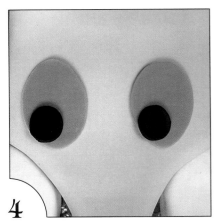

**4**

Roll out, cut and fix sugarpaste eyes as shown.

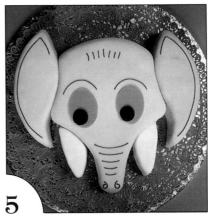

**5**

Using royal icing, pipe the features as shown (No.2).

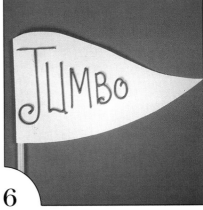

**6**

Using a drinking straw and paper, make the pennant and pipe with inscription of choice (No.1). Fix to the cake board with sugarpaste.

TEMPLATES

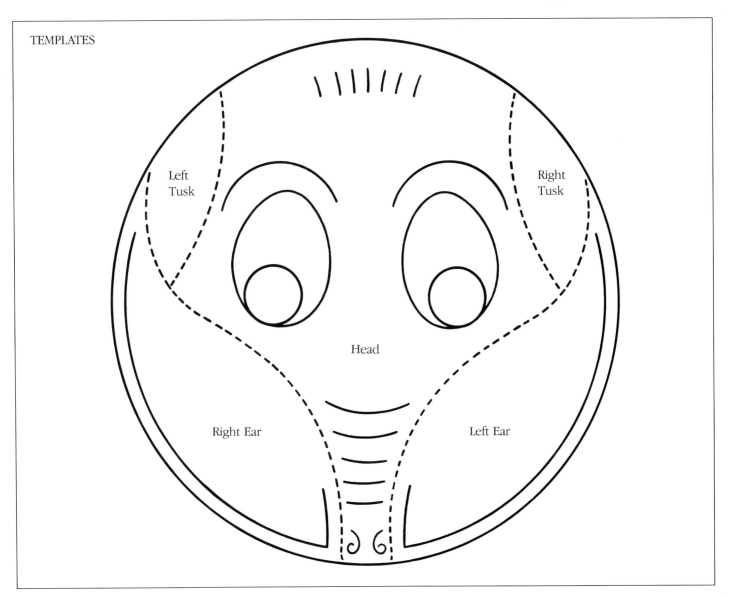

Left Tusk

Right Tusk

Right Ear

Head

Left Ear

# PEPI

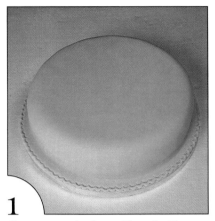

**1**
Cover a round cake and board with sugarpaste and immediately crimp the edge to form a decorative border.

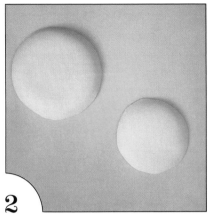

**2**
Cut and form two domed sugarpaste discs, one slightly smaller than the other.

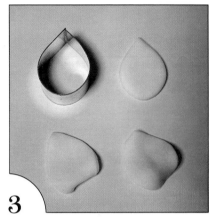

**3**
Using a leaf shaped cutter, cut three sugarpaste petals. Place on a sponge and shape with a modelling tool. Brush with confectioners' dusting powder. 21 required.

**4**
Using royal icing, fix the discs and petals on the cake-top to form flower heads.

**5**
Cut sugarpaste leaves and stems, as shown, and fix in position.

**6**
Decorate flower heads with sugarpaste eyes and piped royal icing features (No.1). Complete decoration with inscription of choice.

TEMPLATES

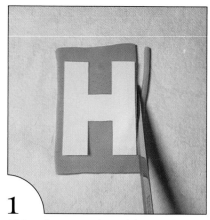

**1** Make a large template of the initial letter. Place on sugarpaste and cut around the template.

**2** Carefully place the initial letter onto the cake-top and fix with cooled, boiled water. Pipe remaining letters in size shown, using royal icing (No.3).

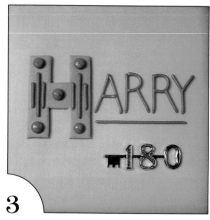

**3** Decorate the initial with piped lines and dots and underline the small letters (No.3). Fix key to cake-top.

**4**

Pipe a rope design along each corner of the cake-top (No.6).

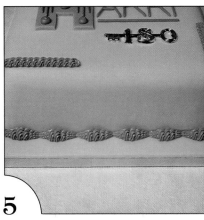

**5**

Divide the cake-base into 6 portions. Pipe a spiral shell into each portion, as shown (No.6).

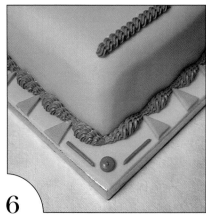

**6**

Roll out, cut and fix sugarpaste triangles between the spiral shells. Pipe lines and a dot at each corner of the cake board (No.3).

TEMPLATES

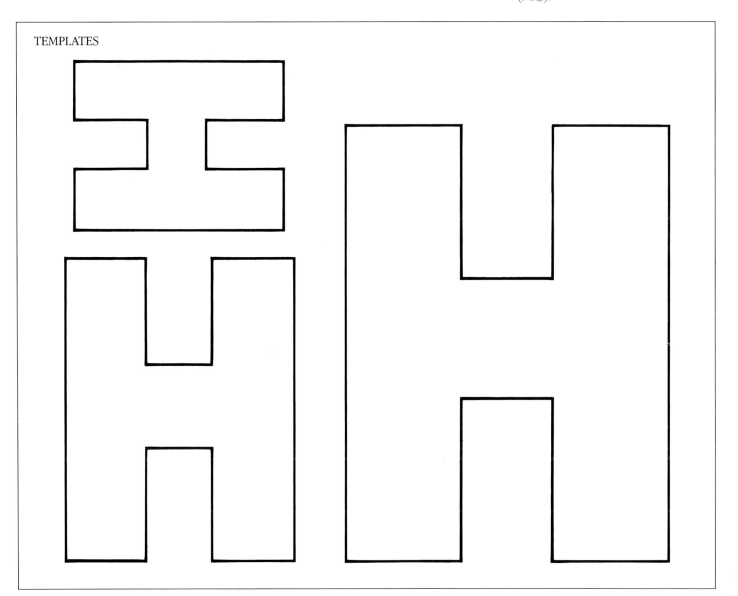

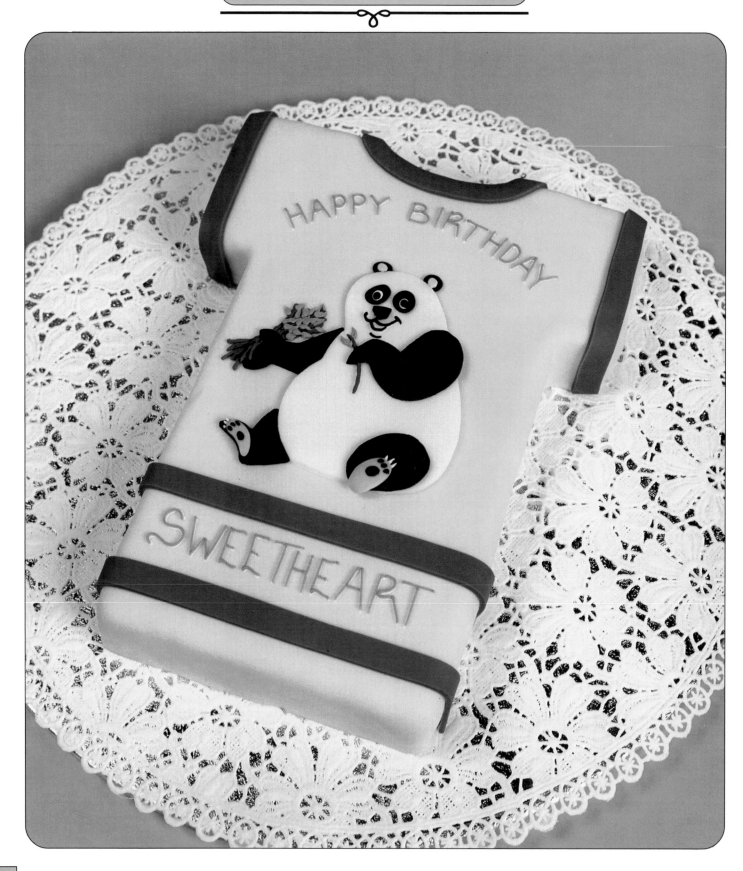

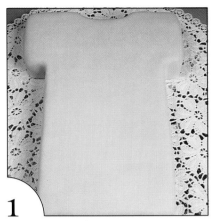

**1** Cut a 20.5cm (8") sponge into the shape of a T-shirt. Cover with sugarpaste and place onto a doyley covered cake board.

**2** Using template as guide, cut out and fix sugarpaste pieces onto the cake-top with cooled, boiled water.

**3** Cut and fix further sugarpaste parts as shown.

**4** Cut and fix sugarpaste feet. Pipe royal icing lines, dots, etc., (No.1) to complete the panda – and then pipe royal icing bamboo shoots.

**5** Cut and fix sugarpaste strips to the T-shirt. Pipe inscription of choice (No.1).

TEMPLATE

**1**

Cover a cake with sugarpaste. Immediately crimp the cake-top edge. Leave to dry for 24 hours.

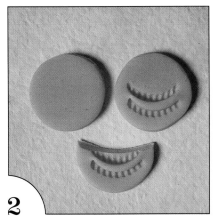

**2**

Cut sugarpaste circles. Crimp the centre and then cut to the crescent shape shown.

**3**

Fix the shapes around the cake board, as shown, using clear alcohol, egg white or cooled, boiled water.

**4**

Cut an L plate from sugarpaste.

**5**

Tear the sugarpaste sign and fix it to the cake-top. Then fix appropriate decorations of choice.

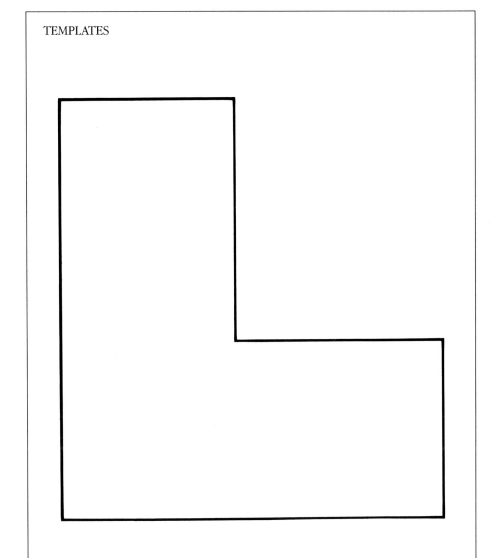

TEMPLATES

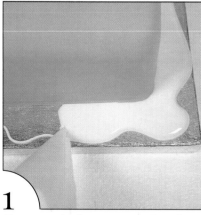

**1**

Place coated cake on a square board. Pipe a wavy line on the board, in royal icing (No.2) and flood-in between cake-base and the line (see p.47). Leave to dry for 24 hours.

**2**

Cut a sugarpaste leaf with leaf cutter or card template. Mark veins with a cocktail stick. Curl to shape. Leave to dry for 24 hours. 14 assorted sized leaves required.

**3**

With royal icing pipe the branch shown on the cake-top (No.3).

**4**

Pipe the owl's body (No.3) on the branch and immediately brush downwards to form feathers using a damp paintbrush.

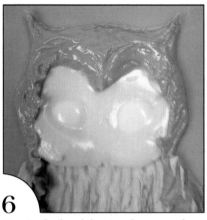

**6**

Pipe-in the head, leaving the eye sockets shallow. Then pipe-in the eye balls. Pipe the head feathers and ears and brush as shown. Pipe the tallons.

**8**

Fix the leaves to the branch using clear alcohol, egg white or cooled, boiled water. Make and fix some sugarpaste stars in the sky.

TEMPLATES

**5**

Pipe the wings and brush inwards to form feathers.

**7**

Paint-in the facial features with edible food colouring. (Note: to avoid colour spreading, mix with an equal amount of clear alcohol.) Make and fix a sugarpaste beak.

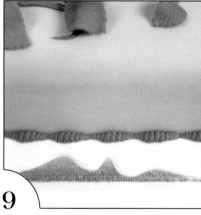

**9**

Pipe spiral scrolls around the cake-base (No.42).

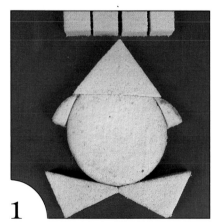

**1** Cut 15cm (6") round and square sponges into shape and position as shown. (Cut as many blocks as required for the name and age.)

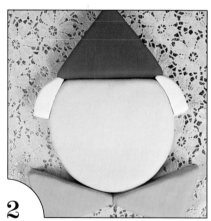

**2** Slice, fill and cover each piece of the clown with buttercream, chill for 1 hour, then cover each piece with sugarpaste. Assemble the clown on a doyley covered board.

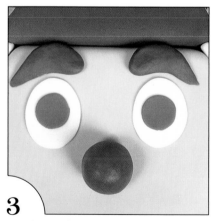

**3** Mould and form sugarpaste eyebrows, eyes and nose and fix into place with royal icing.

**4** Cut and fix sugarpaste pieces to form the mouth and bow tie decoration. Pipe the mouth as shown (No.2).

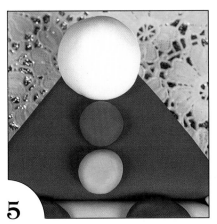

**5** Mould and fix sugarpaste pompoms on the hat.

**6** Cover each block with buttercream and then dip the sides into vermicelli. Cover the top with sugarpaste. Pipe a royal icing letter on each (No.2) and place on cake.

TEMPLATES

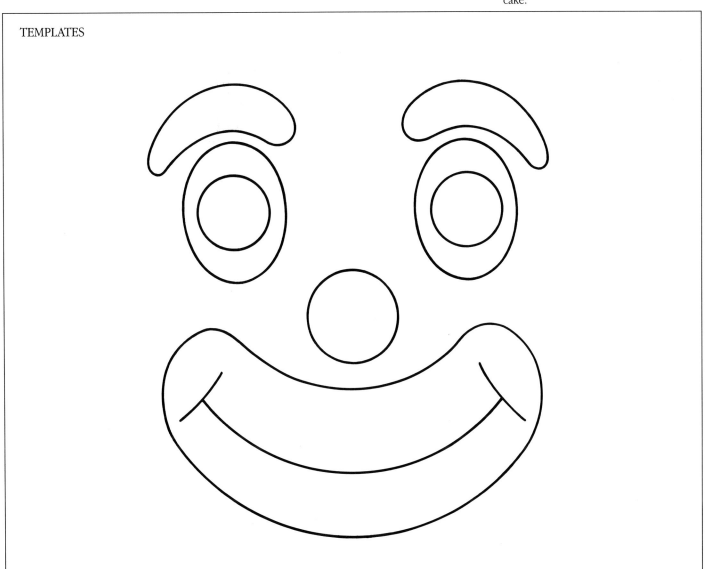

**1**
Outline and flood-in (see p.47) message of choice onto waxed paper (No.1). Leave to dry for 24 hours.

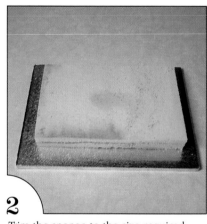

**2**
Trim the sponge to the size required then layer and fill with jam and buttercream.

**3**
Cut the groove along the centre line. Then coat the sponge with a thin layer of buttercream. Place in a refrigerator for 2 hours.

**4** Cover the back and front sides with sugarpaste. Using a knife, mark the paste to form page effect.

**5** Cover the top and ends in one piece of sugarpaste. Using the knife mark the ends, as shown.

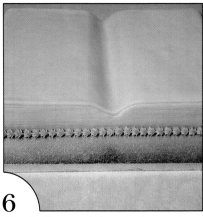

**6** Pipe shells around the cake-base, using royal icing (No.6).

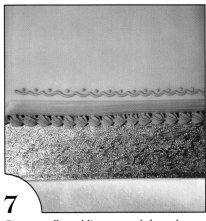

**7** Pipe a scalloped line around the cake-top edge, then pipe the dots shown (No.1).

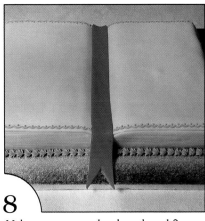

**8** Make a sugarpaste bookmark and fix with royal icing along the centre groove.

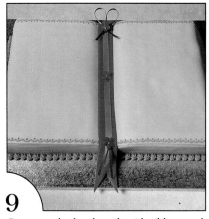

**9** Decorate the bookmark with ribbon and sugarpaste flowers.

**10** Remove the out letters from the waxed paper and fix to one side of the book.

**11** Pipe 'and' to join the two messages together (No.1).

**12** Fix the remaining runout letters to form the second message.

**13**

Fix narrow ribbon strips under the letters, with royal icing, and pipe the lines shown (No.1).

**14**

Repeat step 13, as shown.

**15**

Decorate the corners with bows, flowers and horseshoes. Then pipe the dots (No.1).

TEMPLATES

A B C D E F

G H I J K L

M N O P Q R

S T U V W X

Y Z 1 2 3 4

5 6 7 8 9 0

**1** Cover a cake and board with sugarpaste. Immediately crimp around the edge of the cake board to form the pattern shown.

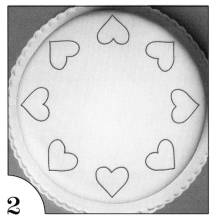

**2** When dry, pipe heart shaped lines evenly round the cake-top edge (No.1) using a template to achieve matching size and shape.

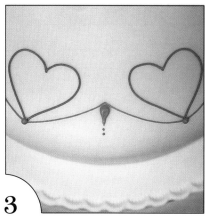

**3** Join each heart with piped lines and dots (No.1). Make and fix sugarpaste rose spray (see p.48). Decorate as required.

# TERRY

**1**

Cut a sugarpaste railroad and fix across a 28cm (11") square cake board with cooled, boiled water. Stipple remainder of board with royal icing.

**2**

Cut and layer sponges to form the shape of a train. Then spread a thin layer of buttercream over the top and sides. Chill for 1 hour in the refrigerator.

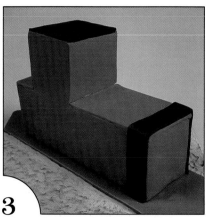

**3**

Cover the sponge with sugarpaste then cut and fix sugarpaste top and front edging with cooled, boiled water. Place the train on the railroad.

**4**

Cut and fix sugarpaste wheels. Then pipe shells around the train's edges (No.43).

**5**

Cut and fix sugarpaste windows, funnel and whistle. Then pipe bulbs on the wheel centres (No.2).

**6**

Cut and fix sugarpaste eyes and nose then decorate features (No.1). Pipe track rails and fix an appropriate plaque onto the grass.

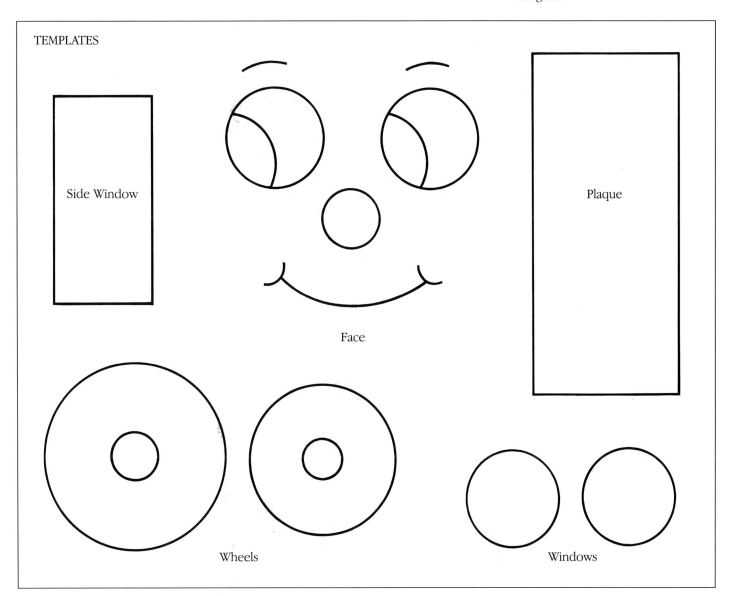

TEMPLATES

Side Window

Plaque

Face

Wheels

Windows

# NANA

**1**

Pipe royal icing shells around the base of a sugarpaste covered heart shaped cake (No.42).

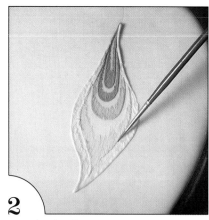

**2**

Transfer the design to the cake-top (see p.54) then, using softened royal icing (see recipe on p.53), brush embroider the part shown.

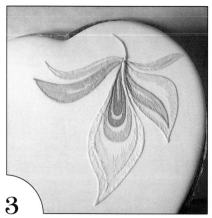

**3**

Continue brush embroidering the flower until complete.

**4**

Pipe the lines and dots shown (No.1). Make and fix a small ribbon bow.

**5**

Pipe inscription of choice onto the cake-top (No.1).

**6**

Decorate the inscription in the manner shown. Then fix a ribbon and bow around the cake-side.

TEMPLATE

# JEREMY

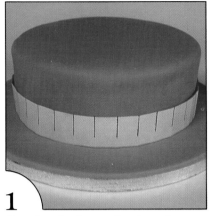

**1** Cut a length of paper the circumference of the cake. Fold it into 32 sections and mark, as shown.

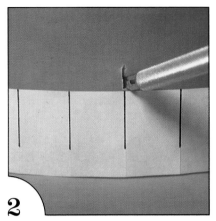

**2** Cut into the sugarpaste, above each marked position on the paper, using a sharp pointed knife.

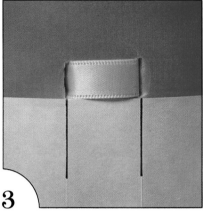

**3** Insert a strip of food-approved ribbon between two cuts, as shown, to form a loop.

**4** Continue to insert ribbon pieces until each section is completed.

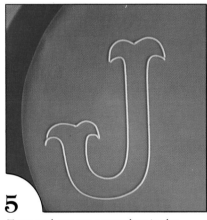

**5** Trace and cut out a template in the initial required. Place it on the cake-top and pipe a line around it with royal icing (No.2).

**6** Carefully remove the template. Decorate initial with piped filigree, dots and petals (No.0).

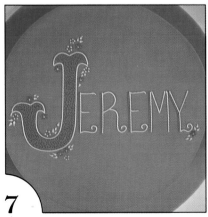

**7** Complete piping name of choice (No.1). Then decorate as shown (No.0).

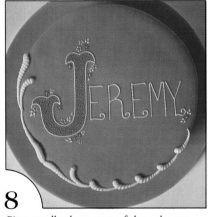

**8** Pipe scrolls along part of the cake-top edge, as shown (No.42).

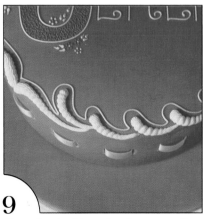

**9** Pipe a line beside each cake-top scroll (No.2).

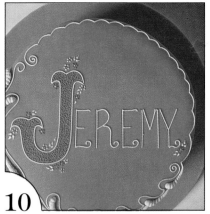

**10** Pipe curved lines around remaining cake-top edge to form the scallop shown (No.2).

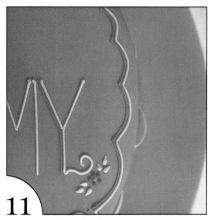

**11** Pipe a line beside the No.2 scalloped line (No.1).

**12** Make, decorate and fix with cooled, boiled water, a sugarpaste birth announcement as shown.

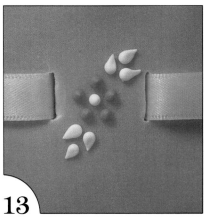

**13** Pipe dots and petals between each cake-side loop (No.2).

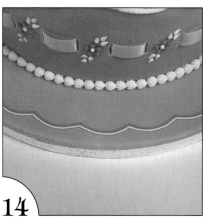

**14** Pipe shells around the cake-base (No.42). Pipe a curved line around the cake board edge (No.2). Then pipe a line beside the No.2 line (No.1).

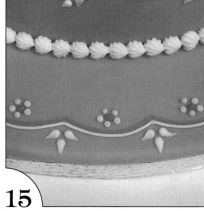

**15** Pipe a circle of dots in the centre of each curve, to form floral motif (No.1). Pipe petal shapes at each curved line join (No.1).

**16** Fix baby to the cake-top and decorate around it with tracery and dots (No.1).

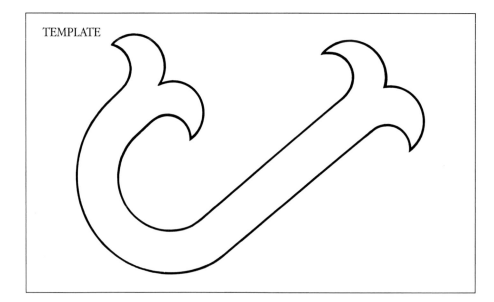

TEMPLATE

# CLARINDA

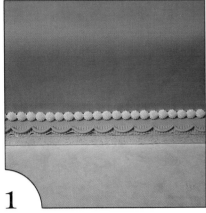

**1** Cover a cake and board in sugarpaste and crimp around the cake board edge. Leave to dry for 24 hours. Using royal icing, pipe shells around the cake-base (No.42).

**2** Fix an floral spray and sugar birds (see p.112) onto the cake-top, as shown, using royal icing.

**3** Pipe the curved lines and graduated dots (No.2). Fix ribbons and decorations of choice to cake-top and base.

# LEONORA

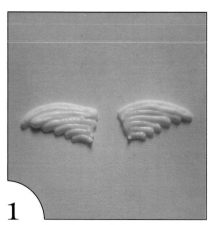

**1**
Pipe a pair of bird's wings onto waxed paper, using royal icing without glycerin (No.1). Leave to dry for 24 hours. 6 sets required.

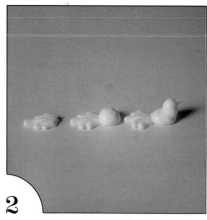

**2**
When the wings are dry, follow the sequence from left to right and pipe the bird's tail, the body and then the head (No.2).

**3**
Immediately fix the wings into the body and, if necessary, support at angle shown until dry.

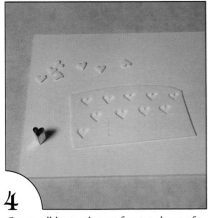

**4**

Cut small heart shapes from a sheet of sugarpaste in a regular pattern, leaving a good space between each heart. Reserve the cut-outs.

**5**

Place the sheet onto green sugarpaste.

**6**

With a larger heart shaped cutter, cut hearts as shown. Leave to dry for 24 hours.

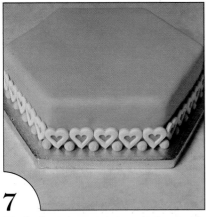

**7**

Fix the hearts around the cake-base with cooled, boiled water. Then pipe a bulb between each heart (No.4).

**8**

Fix the piped sugar birds, small hearts and ribbon bows to the cake-top edge, as shown.

**9**

Using cut strips of thin card as guide, pipe inscription of choice (No.2).

**10**

Overpipe the No.2 lines (No.1).

**11**

Decorate the inscription with piping and small cut-out hearts.

**12**

Fix ribbon to cake board edge and fix small heart in centre of each side. Pipe a dot above each heart (No.1).

# EASTER

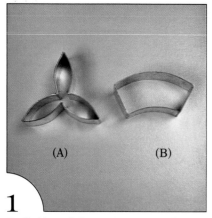

**1**

Daffodil petal shape cutter (A) and trumpet shape cutter (B) required.

**2**

Cut two flower paste petal shapes. Place on a dry household sponge and thin the edges. Mark each petal with a cocktail stick, as shown.

**3**

Moisten the centre of one of the petal shapes with egg white. Immediately join the shapes together to form a flower. Pierce the flower centre with a cocktail stick.

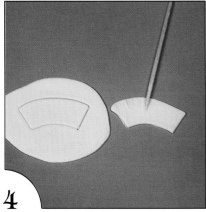

**4**

Cut the shape shown from flower paste. Frill the longer (outer) edge by rolling a cocktail stick backwards and forwards a little at a time.

**5**

Moisten one end with egg white. Join end to end to form a trumpet. Moisten base and fix to the petals. Leave to dry 24 hours. 2 flowers required.

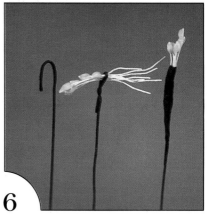

**6**

Cut and bend a length of 24 gauge wire, as shown. Loop and twist the wire over six stamen heads. Fix together in upright position using floral tape.

**7**

Mould a ball of flower paste and insert stem through it. Moisten the inside centre of the flower and insert the stem through the existing hole.

**8**

Pull the stem through the flower until the ball and stamen heads are in the position shown. Then use a cocktail stick to flatten the ball.

**9**

Mould a cone of flower paste and insert the stem through its centre. Moisten the flower base with egg white and fix cone as shown. Leave to dry 24 hours.

**10**

Wind white floral tape around the stem as shown, then coat the tape with edible confectioners' dusting powder.

**11**

Cut and mark two flower paste leaves. Moisten and insert 26 gauge wire into the base of each leaf and then leave to dry in the shape shown for 24 hours.

**12**

To make the spray, place the wired leaves against the flower stems and wrap together with floral tape.

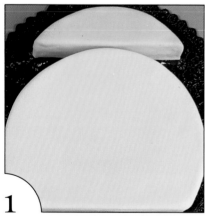

**1** Cut the bottom off a 20.5cm (8") round sponge. Cover pieces in sugarpaste and place on to a doyley and cake board as shown.

**2** Using template as a guide, cut, and fix with cooled, boiled water, a sugarpaste face. Then pipe numerals and features (No.1).

**3** Cut and fix sugarpaste arms, hands, legs and feet.

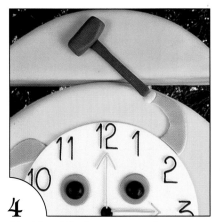

**4** Mould and fix the sugarpaste hammer, then pipe clock hands (No.1).

**5** Pipe WAKEY WAKEY on alarm (No.1).

**6** Cut sugarpaste plaque and place on the doyley, then pipe inscription of choice (No.1) where shown.

TEMPLATES

Face

Hammer

**1**

Cover cakes with sugarpaste to make figures 1 and 8.

**2**

Using template as guide, cut and fix a sugarpaste key and keyhole with cooled, boiled water.

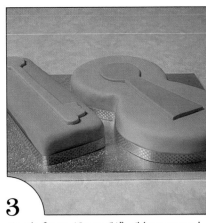

**3**

Neatly fix an 18mm (³/₄") ribbon around each cake-base.

**4**
Pipe HAPPY BIRTHDAY using royal icing (No.2).

**5**
Pipe 18 TODAY onto the keyhole (No.2). Decorate with a cut-out sugarpaste flower.

**6**
Make and fix sugarpaste flowers, to decorate the cakes, as shown.

TEMPLATES

**1** Cover a cake and board with sugarpaste. Then crimp the cake-top edge. Pipe royal icing bulbs around the cake-base (No.2). Leave to dry for 3 days.

**2** Trace template onto greaseproof paper and scribe the design (using a pointed tool) on the cake-top. Then brush embroider (see p.54). Leave to dry for 1 hour.

**3** Pipe bulbs and lines (No.1) onto each flower, to represent flower centres and stamens.

**4**

Pipe a line over each cake-base bulb (No.1). Then fix ribbon around the cake board side (see p.81).

**5**

Pipe inscription of choice on the cake-top and then decorate as shown (Nos.1 and 0).

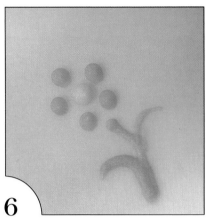

**6**

Pipe the floral design around the cake board and edge (No.2). Pipe scalloped line (No.1). Fix ribbon to cake board side.

**TEMPLATE**

# MICHELLE

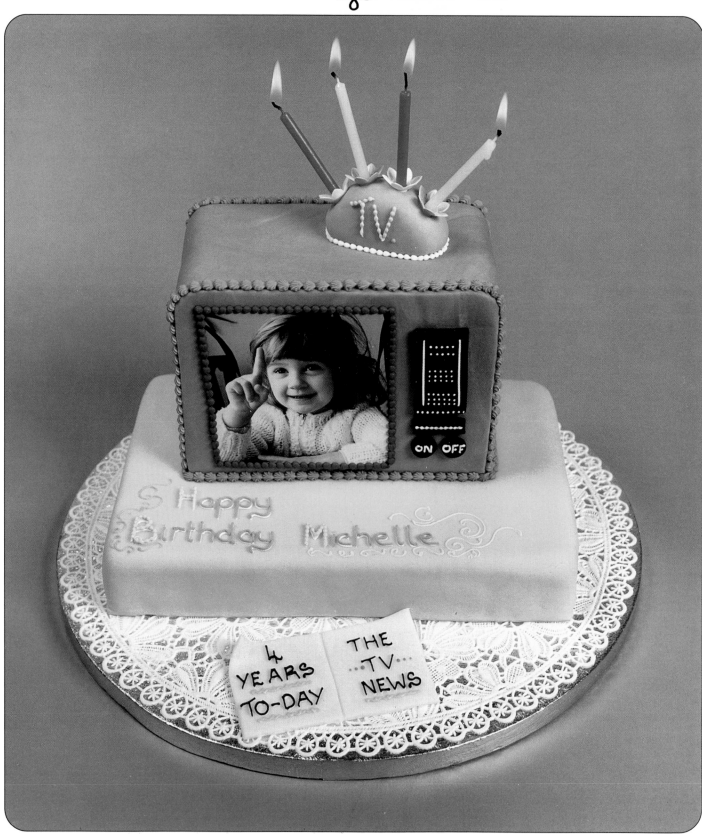

**1** Three 15 x 15cm (6 x 6") sponges are required. Cut two as shown. Place the off-cuts at each side of the third uncut sponge to form the T.V. base.

**2** Slice and fill the T.V. base with buttercream. Chill for 1 hour and then cover with sugarpaste. Place on doyley and board.

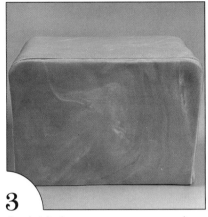

**3** Sandwich the two cut sponges together with buttercream and place in an upright position to form the T.V. Cover in buttercream. Chill for 1 hour and then cover in sugarpaste.

**4** Place T.V. onto the base. Fix a photograph (backed with silver foil) to the front with royal icing. Pipe royal icing shells around the photograph and T.V. edges (No.5).

**5** Roll out, cut and fix with cooled, boiled water, a sugarpaste control panel. Decorate the panel as shown (No.1).

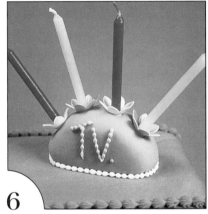

**6** Make and fix a sugarpaste aerial base. Fix candle holders and candles. Then decorate (No.1).

**7** Pipe inscription of choice and tracery (No.1). Cut and place a sugarpaste newspaper on the doyley, then pipe inscription of choice (No.1).

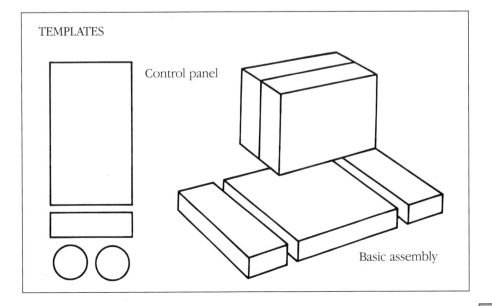

TEMPLATES

Control panel

Basic assembly

**1**

Position the template on the cake-top and then pipe a line around the outside (No.2). Leave to dry for 10 minutes. Carefully remove the template.

**2**

Using template as a guide, pipe in the outline for the eyes, ears, nose and mouth (No.2). Then pipe the paws and back leg.

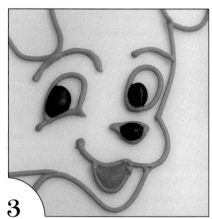

**3**

Pipe-in the eyes, nose and tongue (No.1).

**4** Pipe inscription of choice and the grass around Treacle's feet as shown (No.1).

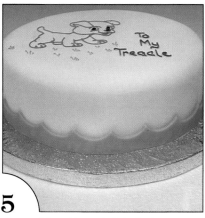

**5** Cut and fix with cooled, boiled water, a sugarpaste scalloped band at cake-base.

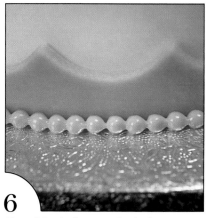

**6** Pipe plain shells around cake-base to complete the decoration (No.2).

TEMPLATES

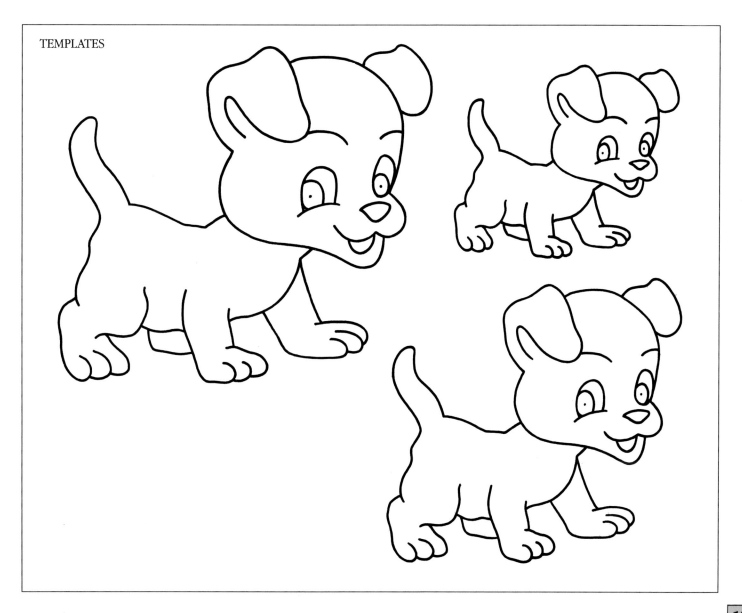

**1** Cover cake and board with sugarpaste. Leave to dry for 24 hours. Cut a narrow strip of paper the circumference of the cake into eight curves and mark side of cake.

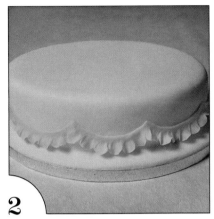

**2** Make a sugarpaste frill (see p.51) and fix to the marked line around the cake-side with cooled, boiled water.

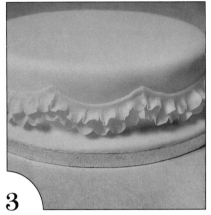

**3** Using a lighter shade of colour repeat step 2 fixing slightly above the first frill to create a double frill.

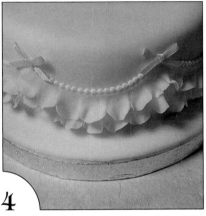

**4** Pipe shells along the top line of the frill, using royal icing (No.2). Make and fix a small bow to each join.

**5** Cut and fix a crimped sugarpaste plaque of appropriate size to the cake-top. Pipe inscription, then overpipe inscription (Nos.2 and 1).

**6** Pipe a series of dots to create floral motifs on the cake-top and board (No.1).

TEMPLATE

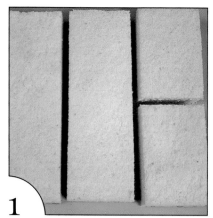

**1** Cut a square sponge into three. Then cut one of the pieces in half, as shown.

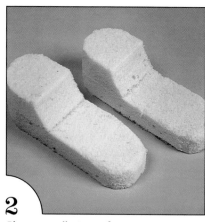

**2** Place a small piece of sponge onto a large one and trim to the shape shown. Repeat with the other two pieces of sponge.

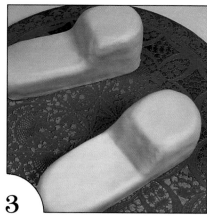

**3** Slice, fill and cover each shoe with buttercream. Chill in refrigerator for 1 hour and then cover with sugarpaste. Place on doyley and board.

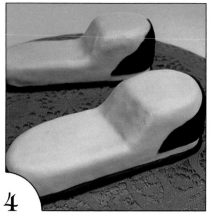

**4** Cut and fix sugarpaste pieces with cooled, boiled water, to form the heel and sole sides.

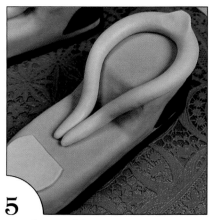

**5** Cut, form and fix sugarpaste sports trainer uppers and toe caps.

**6** Pipe royal icing dashes to represent stitching (No.1).

**7** Pipe royal icing circles to form eye holes (No.1). Then pipe an S (or appropriate initial) on each toe cap (No.3).

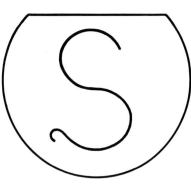

Toe cap

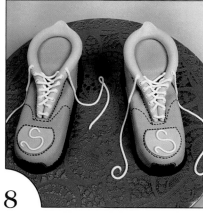

**8** Pipe royal icing laces to complete the decoration (No.3).

TEMPLATES

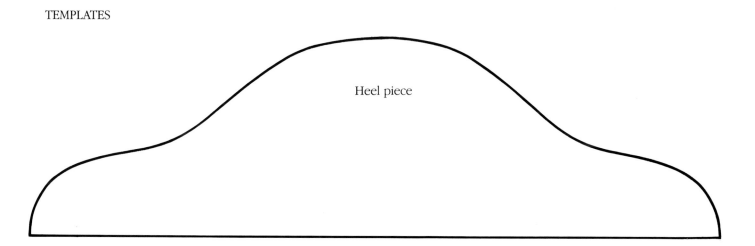

Heel piece

# EDEN

**1**

Mark a circle of paper, slightly smaller than sugarpaste covered board, into six. Using a paint brush, indent paste around edge leaving a space at each mark.

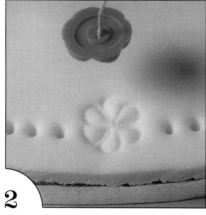

**2**

Using a button with a well defined design, imprint the sugarpaste at each space. Repeat for second board. Leave to dry for 3 days.

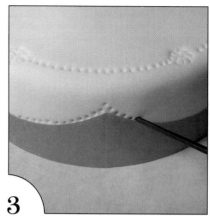

**3**

Repeat steps 1-2 on cake-top. Cut paper, 6.5cm (2½") wide and circumference of cake. Fold into six and cut scallop shape. Unfold, place around cake side and mark as shown.

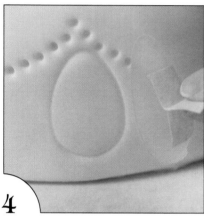

**4**

Cut handle off a 5ml plastic spoon and attach sticky tape to head. Impress into top of each curve. Press button at centre of each design. Leave to dry for 3 days.

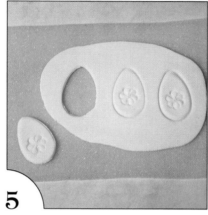

**5**

Roll out sugarpaste to 3mm (⅛") thick. Press spoon head and then button into the paste. Cut out and leave to dry for 3 days on foam or dry flat surface.

**6**

Using diluted food colourings, paint the flower shape petals and centres. Place the cakes onto the sugarpaste covered cake boards.

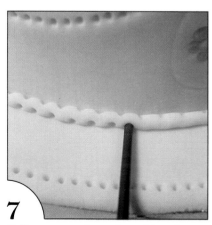

**7**

Roll sugarpaste into a long thin roll. Moisten cake-base with cooled, boiled water and fix roll. Whilst soft, press paint brush into paste to form pattern shown.

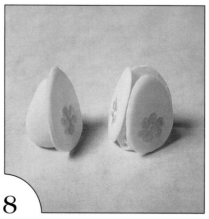

**8**

Form a sugarpaste cone. Moisten and fix the pear shapes to the cone. Leave to dry for 1 hour. Fix the cone into the centre of a cake separator.

**9**

Assemble flowers and leaves, together with decorations to form a spray for the cake-top ornament.

**1** Make template A from thin card to fit cake-side. Sugarpaste the cakes and immediately pin template A to the cake-side. Scratch the outlines.

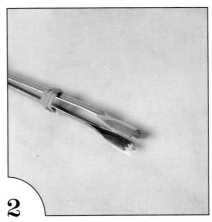

**2** Twist an elastic band around a crimper until it stays open approximately 4.5mm (³/₁₆").

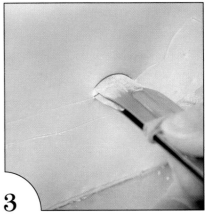

**3** Dip the end of the crimper into icing sugar, tap off excess, then pinch the sugarpaste along the scratch line to form a ridge.

**4** Continue making the ridges in an even thickness and spacing, around each cake-side. Using templates B and C as guides, crimp pattern in cake-top corners.

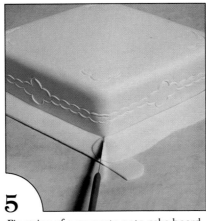

**5** Fix strips of sugarpaste onto cake board with cooled, boiled water. Overlap the corners and cut diagonally, as shown. Remove excess smooth and join.

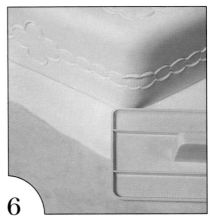

**6** Use a cake smoother to flatten and polish the surface of the sugarpaste around the cake board.

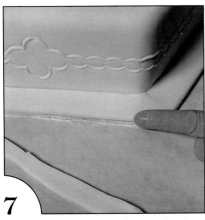

**7** Trim excess sugarpaste along each edge then smooth with a fingertip.

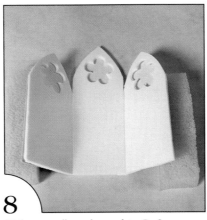

**8** Make a cardboard template D. Score along dotted line and bend. Cut modelling paste (see p.18) to template D. Place over cardboard and leave to dry for 24 hours.

**9** Cut sugarpaste blossoms. Press modelling tool into the centre of each petal on a soft sponge, upturn and press into the flower's centre.

**10** Make a selection of blossoms in various sizes and colours using the method described in step 9.

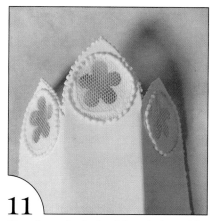

**11** Fix tulle to the back of the window with royal icing. Then pipe shells along the edges, using royal icing (No.0). Leave to dry for 2 hours.

**12** Pipe a line on each section (No.1). Decorate the window with piped stems, leaves and blossoms (No.0).

**13** Fix the window to the cake-top with royal icing, and pipe plain shells around the base (No.2). Leave to dry for 4 hours.

**14** Fix additional blossoms in position shown, then pipe leaves with a leaf bag (see p.45).

**15** Using template E as a guide, cut a diamond shaped card. Cover in board paper and fix onto the cake-top with piped dots (No.2).

**16** Place a cake pillar at each corner and decorate with blossoms and piped leaves.

**17** Fix further small blossoms along the card edge and decorate with piped leaves, as shown.

**18** Fix blossoms to the centre of each cake-side and decorate with piped leaves. Pipe shells around the cake-base (No.2). Fix ribbon around board edge.

TEMPLATES

D

A

B

C

E

NOTE: Half template
only. Place on folded
paper. Open out before
using to cut cardboard
template.

**1**

Cut and shape a piece of sugarpaste into an oblong. Then, using a palette knife, press down the centre to form a book.

**2**

Mark the side to create page effect and cut a thin slice at the top right-hand corner for a leaf.

**3**

Place the book onto a sugarpaste cover. Decorate with a bookmark then pipe inscription using royal icing (No.1).

**4**

Crystallise a freshly-cut carnation (see p.58). Leave until dry.

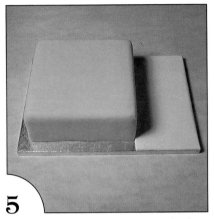

**5**

Place a square sugarpaste covered cake onto an oblong board. Then cover remaining area with sugarpaste, fixing with cooled, boiled water.

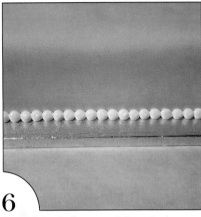

**6**

Pipe plain shells around the cake-base (No.3).

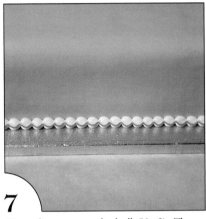

**7**

Pipe a line over each shell (No.2). Then overpipe the No.2 line (No.1).

**8**

Fix the book in position with royal icing, then a pair of rings and doves.

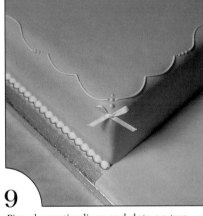

**9**

Pipe decorative lines and dots on two edges of the cake-top (No.2). Fix a ribbon bow on the corner.

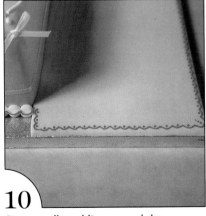

**10**

Pipe a scalloped line around the sugarpaste and a dot in each curve (No.1) as shown.

**11**

Carefully fix the carnation and fern as shown, using dots of royal icing.

**12**

Decorate the stem with graduated ribbon bows and piped dots.

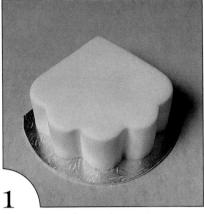

**1**
Cut mature cakes to shape using template A. Cover with sugarpaste. Fix to boards, referring to template F for shape of middle tier board.

**2**
Use flowers or, with templates B, C & D, make 2 large flower paste orchids (see p.148), 20 blossoms on 28 gauge wire, small unwired blossoms, and 7 butterflies.

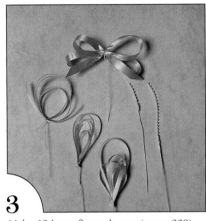

**3**
Make 12 large finger loops (see p.229). Twist wire around base. Cover wires with tape. Make 2 double bows. Tape lengths of pearl strings to 24 guage wires.

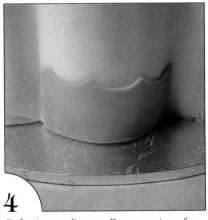

**4**
Referring to diagram E, cut sections for border from flower paste, adjusting length of each section as necessary. Moisten with cooled, boiled water and fix.

**5**
Add further sections, making joins as neat as possible. Complete borders around all four cakes.

**6**
Pipe scallops (No.1) just below top-edge of border. Pipe dots to points of scallops and border as shown. Pipe shells (No.42) around cake-base.

**7**
Mark guide lines on top tier. Pipe royal icing line on inner guide line (No.2). Fix pearls. Take pearls over edge and fix with royal icing, overlapping border.

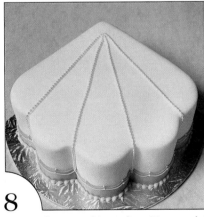

**8**
Repeat for second inner line. Pipe royal icing lines over both outer guide lines and fix pearls in one continuous strip.

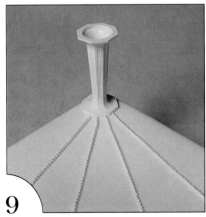

**9**
Mark pillar positions on middle and bottom tiers. Fix pearls to middle tiers as in steps 7 and 8. Fix pearls to bottom tier leaving space for central pillar.

**139**

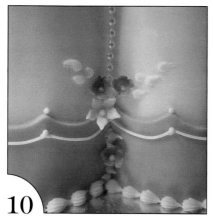

**10**

Fix blossoms and piped leaves (No.1) to conceal end of pearl strings and join in border section. Fix blossoms to conceal join between the sections.

**11**

Tape up flower sprays using prepared materials or artificial flowers. Tape together blossoms, ribbons, etc, first.

**12**

Very carefully pull-in orchid to prevent breaking. Tape wires together. Neaten back of spray with double bow.

**13**

Fix spray to top tier. Fix one butterfly. Tape up second flower spray and reserve.

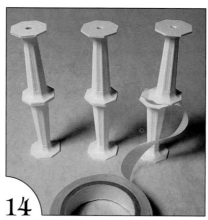

**14**

Fix together 2 pillars with double sided sticky tape to form a double pillar. 3 double pillars required.

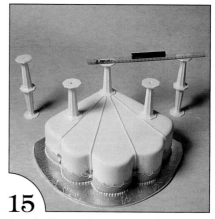

**15**

Stand pillars on bottom tier, place double pillars in position either side. Check levels and adjust if necessary. Insert skewers.

**16**

Place middle tier in position. Fix pillar to board at centre back. Position pillars. Check levels and adjust. Remove to insert skewers. Fix butterflies.

**17**

Position flower spray on bottom tier and fix with royal icing. Add one butterfly.

**18**

Complete by placing top tier in position.

TEMPLATES

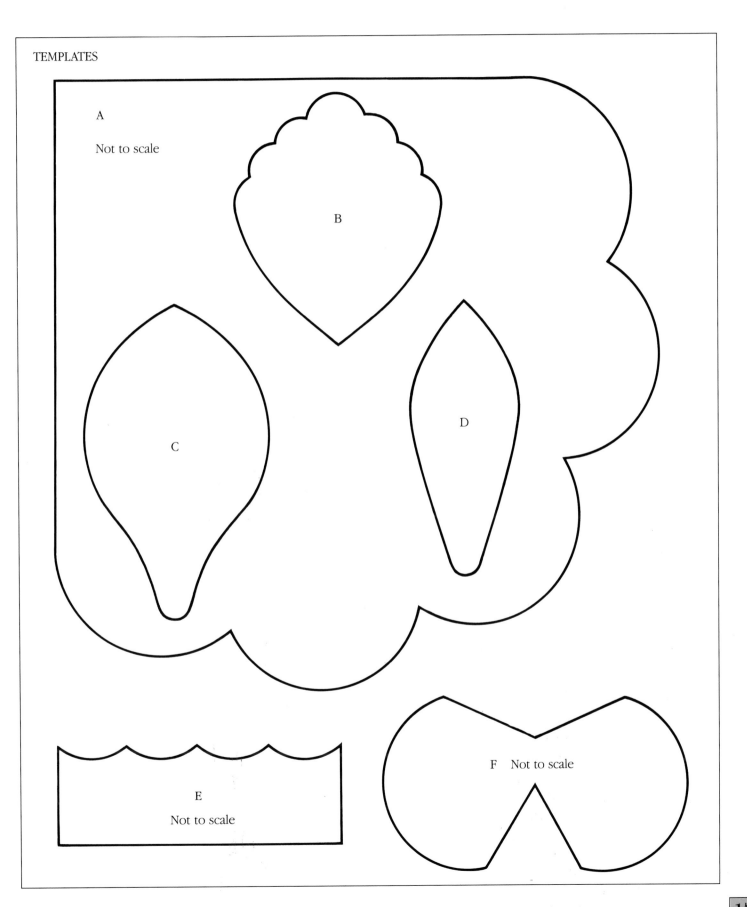

A

Not to scale

B

C

D

E

Not to scale

F    Not to scale

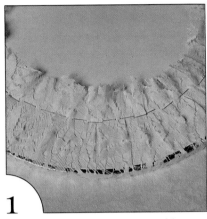

**1**

Using net, cover board and roughly tape to back. Staple around inside edge, as the net is gathered. Trim away surplus from centre. Cover with a thin board for top tier.

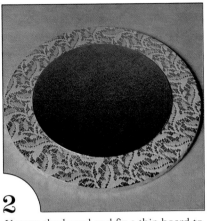

**2**

Upturn the board and fix a thin board to the top (the same size as the cake). Repeat steps 1-2 for second cake board. Cover cakes in sugarpaste and place in centre of cake boards.

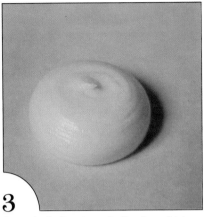

**3**

To make bells, pipe a bulb of royal icing (without glycerin) onto waxed paper (No.4).

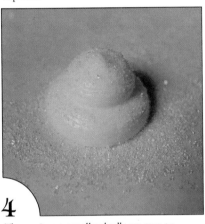

**4**

Then pipe a smaller bulb on top to create a cottage loaf shape. Immediately sprinkle granulated sugar over top and sides. 3 required. Leave to dry for 3 to 4 hours.

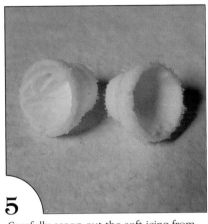

**5**

Carefully scoop out the soft icing from the centre of the bells. Leave to dry for 24 hours.

**6**

Cut and fix sugarpaste shapes for cake-base, using a brush moistened with pure alcohol or cooled boiled water. Repeat with different shape for cake-top edge.

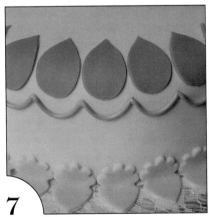

**7**

Pipe a scalloped line around the cake-side (No.3).

**8**

Pipe a bulb at the centre of each cake-base cut-out (No.3).

**9**

Fix the sugar bells with royal icing. Pipe cords and clangers (No.2). Decorate cakes with ribbons, bows and decorations of choice. Fix a bridal couple to the cake-top.

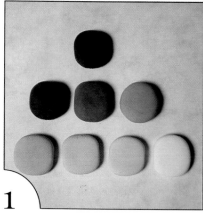

**1**

Make and number 8 colour samples of sugarpaste, from deepest shade no.1 of colour required to white no.8. Colour bulk sugarpaste to match no's.4 and 8.

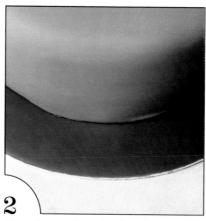

**2**

Cover bottom board with no.1. Leave 24 hours. Cover bottom cake with no.4. Fix to board. Knead ½ tsp gum tragacanth into 60g (2oz) sugarpaste no.4 and reserve.

**3**

Cover top cake with no.8. Leave 24 hours. Knead ½ tsp gum tragacanth into 60g (2oz) no.8 sugarpaste and reserve. Referring to template, scratch mark cake-sides.

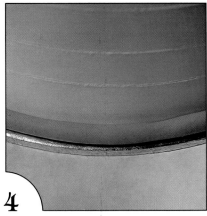

**4**

Place top tier cake onto a 12mm (½")
larger thin board. Fix a long thin roll of
paste to each cake-base; no.1 for bottom
tier; no.5 for top tier.

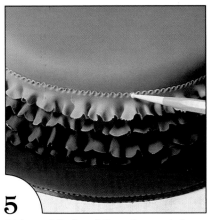

**5**

Make and fix four frills, colour no's.1 to
4, around side of bottom tier. Indent
edge of top frill with modelling tool to
neaten.

**6**

Stand top tier on a spare cake board.
Make and fix frill, colour no.5,
concealing the thin board. Make and fix
frills, colour no's 6 to 8. Neaten top frill.

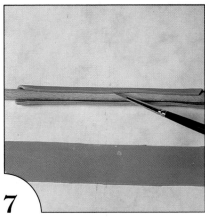

**7**

Roll out reserved paste no.4 and wrap
around a skewer dusted with cornflour.
Carefully moisten edges and join
together.

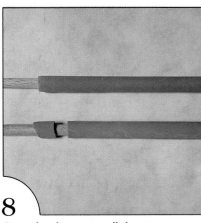

**8**

Press the skewer to roll the paste
smooth. Cut paste to 9cm (3½") long.
3 required.

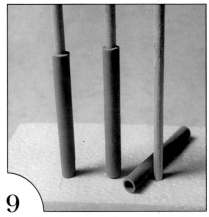

**9**

Dry pillars in an upright position. When
dry enough to hold own shape remove
skewers and leave to dry a further 24
hours.

**10**

Dust a 5cm (2") diameter mould with
cornflour. Join a strip, reserved colour
no.8, 18mm (¾") wide around base. Dry,
remove mould, dry for further 24 hours.

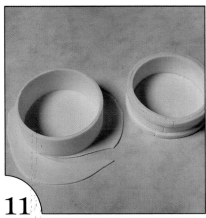

**11**

Moisten bottom edge of ring and fix to
rolled out matching paste, and trim. Cut
and fix narrow strips to top and bottom
edges (staggering the joins).

**12**

Repeat steps 10 and 11, making a ring
4cm (1½") diameter and 2.5cm (1")
high. Fix large ring onto small. Paint
container and pillars with edible varnish.

**13**
Insert skewers (see p.27) into bottom tier. Tape several 24 gauge wires together. Begin to tape artificial flowers and leaves to wires.

**14**
Add more flowers to the wire and then bend to form a ring. (3 required). Tape ends together and conceal with more flowers and leaves. Place over pillars.

**15**
Fill container with artificial flowers and leaves to tone with shade no.8. Fix to the top tier. Assemble, removing spare cake board.

TEMPLATES

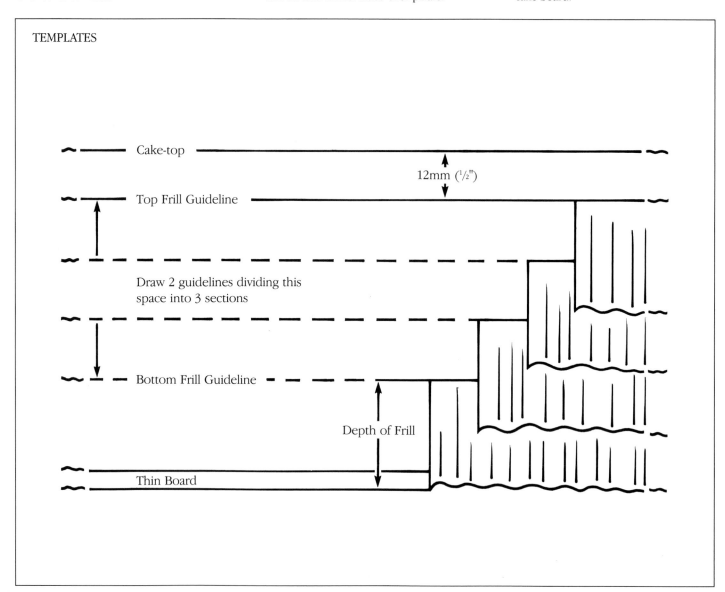

Cake-top

12mm (½")

Top Frill Guideline

Draw 2 guidelines dividing this space into 3 sections

Bottom Frill Guideline

Depth of Frill

Thin Board

**1**

Cover appropriate sized cake boards with sugarpaste. Leave to dry for 24 hours.

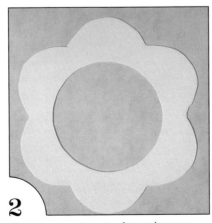

**2**

Using appropriate sized templates cut modelling paste collars (see p.18), as shown. Leave to dry 12 hours. Upturn and leave to dry for a further 24 hours.

**3**

Cover the cake-tops in white sugarpaste and the sides in colour of choice. Fix to the covered boards. Leave to dry for 24 hours.

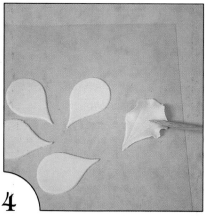

**4** Using template as a guide, cut 5 Azalea petals from flower paste. Vein and frill by rolling a cocktail stick backwards and forwards along the edge.

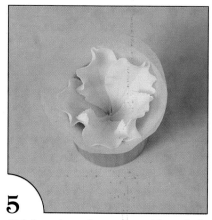

**5** Lightly moisten the overlap with cooled, boiled water and fix four petals in cone shaped mould. Fix last petal as shown. Leave to dry for 12 hours. 15 required.

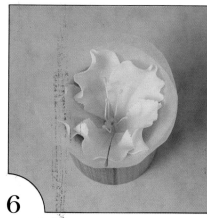

**6** Fix 5 short and 1 long stamen into the centre of each flower with royal icing.

**7** Colour the flowers with confectioners' dusting powder and edible food colouring.

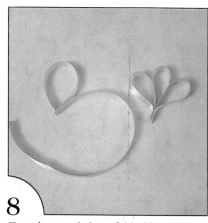

**8** To make a triple bow, fold ribbon into a loop holding between finger and thumb. Fold twice more and cut off spare ribbon.

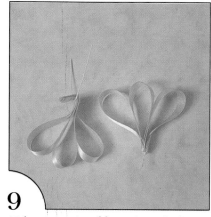

**9** Make a quantity of finger loops by laying 28 gauge wire over ribbon end. Fold ribbon over wire and then twist wire to secure. Trim wire as required.

**10** Fold and secure ribbon to make a single loop and tail. Twist wire as in step 9. 12 required.

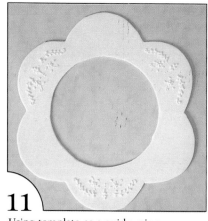

**11** Using template as a guide, pipe embroidery on three alternate sides of the collar (No.1).

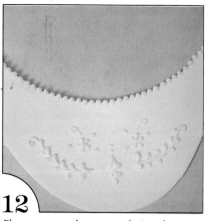

**12** Place on waxed paper and pipe dots around the inside edge (No.2).

**13**
Pipe embroidery on alternate columns around the cake-side (No.1). Pipe shells around the cake-base (No.2).

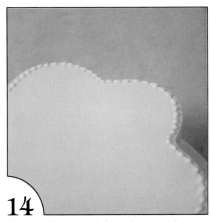

**14**
Pipe shells around the cake-top edge (No.3).

**15**
Immediately fix the collar to the cake-top with royal icing.

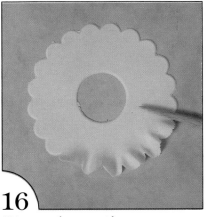

**16**
Using template as guide, cut a sugarpaste disc on a cornflour dusted surface. Start to frill the edge using a cocktail stick.

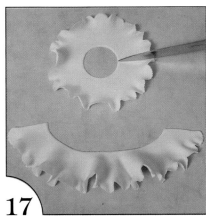

**17**
Complete the frilling, then cut the disc once and pull apart.

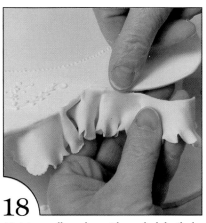

**18**
Moisten collar edge with cooled, boiled water or egg white. Supporting the frill with one hand, press top edge of frill firmly onto moistened collar edge to fix.

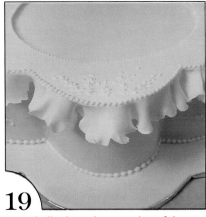

**19**
Pipe shells along the top-edge of the collar (No.2) to neaten join.

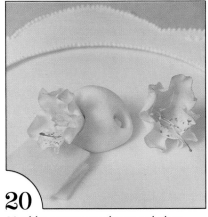

**20**
Mould a sugarpaste dome and place onto the cake-top. Using a blunt-ended tool, indent holes and fix flowers (support on sponge until dry).

**21**
Complete the top spray with additional flowers and then insert ribbon bows, concealing the sugarpaste dome.

TEMPLATES

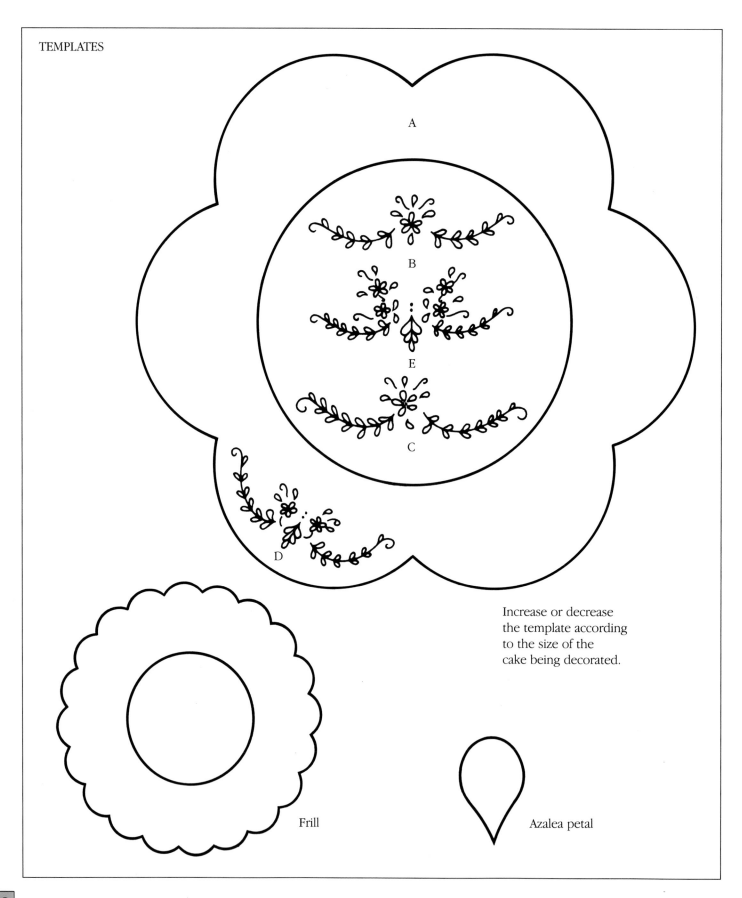

Increase or decrease
the template according
to the size of the
cake being decorated.

Frill

Azalea petal

**1**

Place template on cake-top then stipple edge (see p.160). Repeat for cake-side with scalloped template to fit side. Stipple board. Fix ribbons around cake-base.

**2**

Pipe the season's message following the curved shaped (No.2). Then overpipe the message (No.1).

**3**

Fix sugar bells (see p.143) and narrow ribbon bows around the cake-top. Fix decorative ribbon around the cake board edge.

# MERRY CHRISTMAS

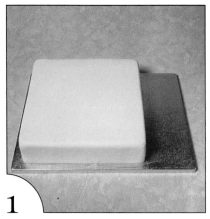

**1**

Cover a square cake with sugarpaste and place on an oblong cake board.

**2**

Using templates as guide, cut the various parts shown from modelling paste (see p.18). Leave until dry.

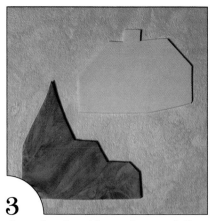

**3**

Cut a church and house from modelling paste. Then mountains and trees as required. Leave until dry.

**4**

Assemble and decorate, with royal icing, Father Christmas and the snowman (No.1). Leave to dry for 24 hours.

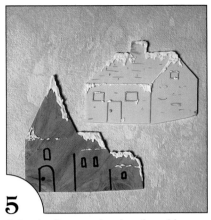

**5**

Paint the lines on the church and house with edible food colouring, then pipe the snow (No.1). Leave to dry for 24 hours.

**6**

Decorate the trees as shown. Leave to dry for 24 hours.

**7**

Decorate the mountains as shown. Leave to dry for 24 hours.

**8**

Cut a sugarpaste plaque and fix Christmas motif. Leave to dry for 24 hours.

**9**

Stipple the cake-top with royal icing to create snow effect. Fix the large mountain to the back of the cake using royal icing.

**10**

Fix the other pieces as shown using royal icing.

**11**

Fix the remaining pieces onto the cake-top.

**12**

Fix plaque to cake board, with royal icing, and decorate with ribbons and bows.

TEMPLATES

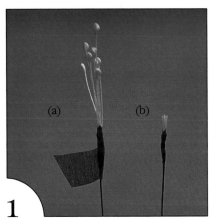

**1**

(a) Fold four stamens in half and twist 24 gauge wire around the centre. Tape the join as shown. (b) Cut stamen heads off approximately 5mm (¼") above the tape.

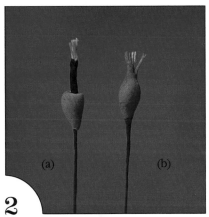

**2**

(a) Mould a cone from flower paste. Moisten tape with egg white and insert wire into cone. (b) Mould cone as shown. Leave to dry for 24 hours.

**3**

Repeat steps 1-2 to form six more flower heads. Pipe two royal icing dots on each flower head (No.1). Leave to dry for 1 hour. Bind stems together with tape.

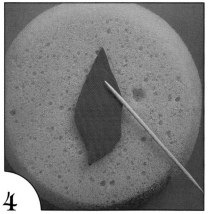

**4**

Using template as guide, cut a leaf from thinly rolled flower paste. Place leaf on a household sponge and mark veins with light pressure from a cocktail stick.

**5**

Cut a length of 26 gauge wire and lay on leaf. Pinch moistened leaf base on to wire. Leave to dry for 24 hours. Repeat steps 5-7 for the required number of leaf shapes.

**6**

Brush leaves and flower heads with confectioners' dusting powder. Tape A leaves to the flower stem. Then tape B leaves, followed by C leaves.

**7**

Continue taping D leaves to the stem. Then add E leaves and finally the green E leaves to complete the flower.

**8**

Cover cake with sugarpaste and carefully crimp the edge on the cake board.

**9**

Fix the spray in a suitable position with royal icing. Pipe Christmas, or inscription of choice (No.2).

**10**

Carefully overpipe the inscription (No.1) in a strong dark colour.

**11**

Pipe beside the inscription, as shown (No.0). Then pipe holly leaves and berries as shown in the main picture (No.0).

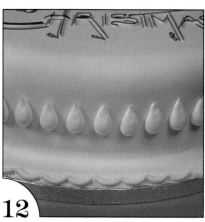

**12**

Pipe large, plain elongated shells evenly spaced around the middle of the cake-side (No.3).

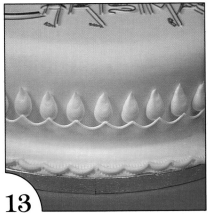

**13**

Pipe a line at the base of each shell to join shell with loops (No.2).

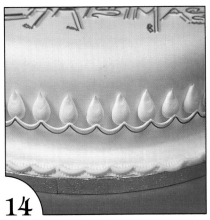

**14**

Pipe a second line below the first line to form another row of loops (No.1). Attach at top of each loop.

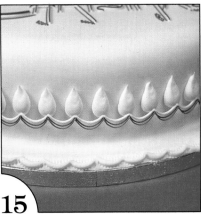

**15**

Pipe a third row of loops below the second (No.1). Attach at top of each loop.

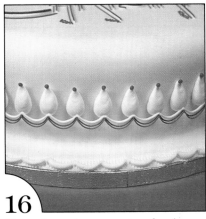

**16**

Pipe a dot at the top centre of each cake-side shell (No.1).

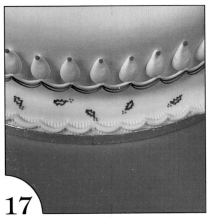

**17**

Pipe the outline of small holly leaves and then dots for berries around the cake board (No.0).

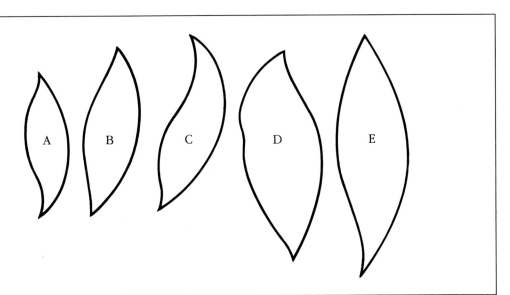

**18**

Make and fix a sugarpaste log to the cake-top. Decorate with piped snow and robins. Fix ribbon around the cake board edge to complete the cake.

TEMPLATES

Number of leaves required:
Shape A x 4 red
Shape B x 2 red
Shape C x 2 red
Shape D x 3 red
Shape E x 3 red
Shape E x 3 green

A metal or plastic cutter in each of the shapes shown is required. If a cutter is not available, the shape can be traced on to card and used as a template.

A    B    C    D    E

# CHRISTMAS ROSE

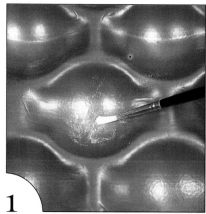

**1**

Dust the centre of a suitable mould (e.g. a smooth apple tray) with cornflour.

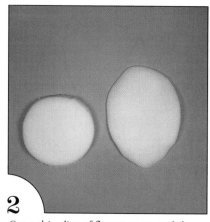

**2**

Cut a thin disc of flower paste and then immediately flatten the edge. This forms a petal. 5 petals required for each flower.

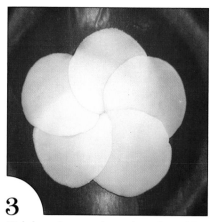

**3**

Lightly moisten each petal overlap with cooled, boiled water and interlock the five petals in the mould, as shown.

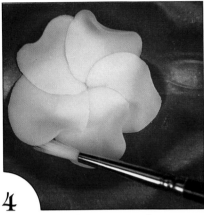

**4**
Curl each petal (using a cornflour dusted paint brush). 9 flowers required. Leave to dry for 24 hours. Then brush with confectioners' dusting powder.

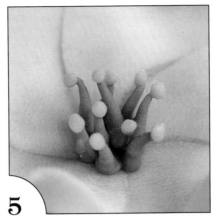

**5**
Pipe stamens to the centre of each Christmas rose (No.1). Then pipe an anther on to each stamen. Leave to dry for 12 hours.

**6**
Carefully remove each Christmas Rose from its mould and leave to thoroughly dry on greaseproof paper.

**7**
Roll out, cut and place flower paste holly leaves on a rounded mould (e.g. a dowel). 50 leaves of varying sizes required. Leave to dry for 24 hours.

**8**
Roll out and fix with cooled, boiled water, a sugarpaste rope around cake-base. Immediately mark the rope with a fork. Make and fix sugarpaste shoots.

**9**
Brush some softened royal icing along the branch to create a snow effect.

**10**
Fix the Christmas Roses to the cake-top centre with royal icing. Paint veins on prepared holly leaves with edible food colour and fix to the cake-top, as shown.

**11**
Pipe groups of royal icing berries where shown (No.1).

**12**
Fix remaining holly leaves along the tree branch. Pipe berries amongst the holly leaves. Secure ribbon to cake board edge.

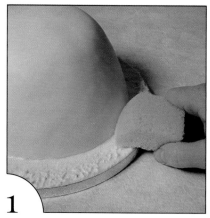

**1** Cover a pudding basin shaped cake with sugarpaste. Place onto cake board. Leave to dry. Spread royal icing (with glycerin) on cake board and then stipple with a fine sponge.

**2** Fix party hat to top of cake with royal icing. Cut and fix sugarpaste eyes, nose and mouth. Fix collar and knot around base.

**3** Stipple snow on hat. Make and fix sugarpaste holly leaves and berry. Fix a motto and robin.

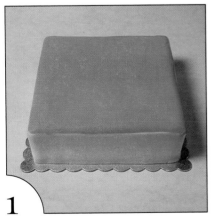

**1**
Cover cake with almond paste. Leave to dry for 24 hours, then cover top only with sugarpaste. Leave to dry for 24 hours.

**2**
Frill (see p.51) and fix sugarpaste pieces with cooled, boiled water, as shown.

**3**
Decorate the cake with ribbon bows and seasonal decorations. Fix band around cake-side.

161

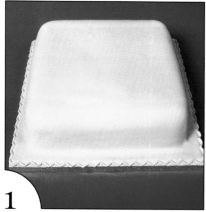

**1** Cover the cake and board with sugarpaste and immediately crimp around the board edge, as shown.

**2** Outline and flood-in a holly leaf on waxed paper, using template as guide (No.1). Leave to dry for 24 hours then paint the veins. 30 required.

**3** Pipe the poinsettia leaves on waxed paper, using template as a guide (No.2). Leave to dry for 2 hours. 8 required.

**4** Pipe-in the centre of each poinsettia, as shown (No.1). Leave to dry for 24 hours.

**5** Stipple the part of the cake-top and corners shown with royal icing and a fine sponge. Leave to dry for 2 hours.

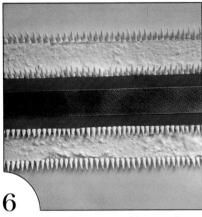

**6** Fix a wide and a narrow ribbon to the cake-top with royal icing. Pipe icicles on the ribbon edges and against the stippled edges (No.1).

**7** Pipe curved lines on the cake-top corners as shown (No.2).

**8** Fix three poinsettias to each piped design.

**9** Fix holly leaves to each piped design.

**10** Pipe berries at the base of each leaf, as shown (No.1).

**11** Pipe curved lines around the cake-base (No.2). Then decorate with poinsettias, leaves and berries.

TEMPLATES

# CHRISTABEL

**1**
Use artificial flowers, or make 20 Winter Jasmine flowers and 10 buds (see p.50), 12 holly leaves and berries, and 25 ivy leaves from flower paste.

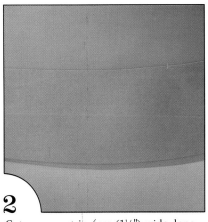

**2**
Cut a paper strip 4cm (1½") wide, long enough to surround the cake. Mark every 5cm (2") along the top-edge. Fit strip around cake-side and transfer marks.

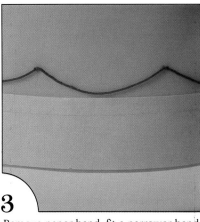

**3**
Remove paper band, fit a narrower band below marks. Pipe loops as shown (No.1) with royal icing.

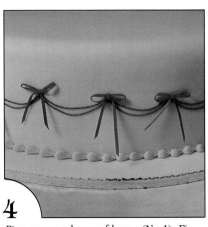

**4**
Pipe a second row of loops (No.1). Fix bows made with 1.5mm wide ribbon. Pipe shells around the cake-base (No.42). Fix silver band around cake board edge.

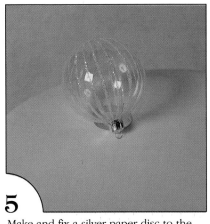

**5**
Make and fix a silver paper disc to the large cake-top. Fix a clear ornament to the disc, using royal icing.

**6**
Make and fix two sprays using flowers, leaves and ribbon loops.

**7**
Repeat steps 5 to 6 for the middle tier cake, as shown.

**8**
Decorate a Perspex cake-top stand with flowers, leaves and ribbon loops.

**9**
Decorate cake stand with ribbon. Fix a thin cake card, slightly smaller than the top tier board, and attach baubles. Assemble cake as shown in main picture.

**1**

Form and fix a sugarpaste cone to the top of a flower nail and immediately snip the cone to form a Christmas tree. 1 large and 6 small required.

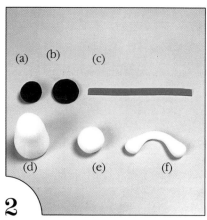

(a) (b) (c)

(d) (e) (f)

**2**

Cut and form the sugarpaste shapes required:
(a) hat crown; (b) hat rim;
(c) scarf; (d) body;
(e) head; (f) arms.

**3**

Fix the shapes, using royal icing, to make a snowman. 6 required. Decorate trees and snowmen with piped snow. Decorate cake as shown in main picture.

# PIPING GEL

Piping gel, which is suitable for use on royal iced, sugarpaste or buttercream-coated cakes, is a very easy medium to use for cake decoration. It is ideal for beginners or busy mums who need an instant effect, and is also suitable for children. Its shiny, transparent finish can be colourful or delicate according to the colours chosen.

The basic clear gel (available from cake decorating suppliers) can be coloured using liquid or paste food colours, but many supermarkets now stock tubes of ready-coloured gel. The basic ready-made colours can be mixed to give further subtle shading. Bear in mind, when mixing, that piping gel really is a medium where a very little goes a long way. A tile, plate or marble slab makes an excellent palette for mixing colours. The gel should then be tranferred to a small piping bag without a tube. Several bags will be needed for most designs.

When working, each section to be coloured should be completely outlined in royal icing (No.1) or piping chocolate to avoid seepage of colour. Then carefully pipe-in the coloured gel. You can then move onto the next area of colour without any time for drying. Alternatively, piping gel can be spread or piped in small dots of colour without the need for an outline, as on the cake on page 171.

## Piping Chocolate

Piping chocolate can be made by mixing a few drops of water into chocolate that has been melted in a bowl over hot water. Alternatively, slowly add approximately $\frac{1}{4}$ teaspoon of glycerin into 115g (4oz) melted chocolate, stirring continuously, until desired consistency is reached. Keep spare piping chocolate warm by standing bowl in a basin of warm water.

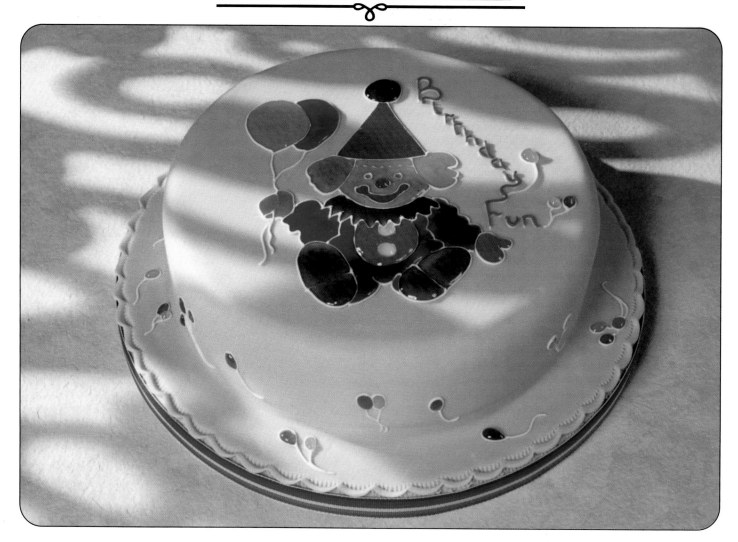

**1**

Cover sponge and cake board in sugarpaste and immediately crimp the edge. Leave to dry for 12 hours. Trace clown onto the cake-top with a confectioners' pen.

**2**

Carefully pipe all the lines using royal icing (No.1).

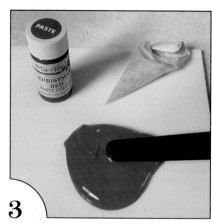

**3**

Thoroughly mix food colour into piping gel, using a palette knife. Fill each colour into a separate piping bag without a piping tube.

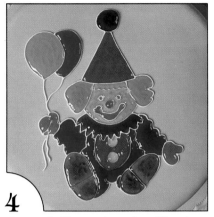

**4**
Snip end off piping bags then fill-in the clown, using the coloured piping gel, keeping the gel shallow.

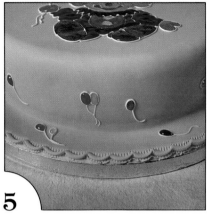

**5**
Pipe balloons and string around the cake-side and board (No.1) with royal icing. Then fill-in the balloons using the coloured piping gel.

**6**
Using royal icing, pipe message of choice (No.1) and then decorate with more balloons.

TEMPLATE

**1** Two round sponge cakes of the same size are required. Cut one sponge cake one-third across the width as shown.

**2** Place the pieces together, on a hexagonal cake board, to form the shape shown. Layer and coat with buttercream. Chill for 1 hour.

**3** Carefully cover the cake with a thin layer of sugarpaste, easing the paste into the steps.

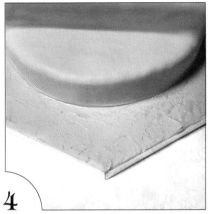

**4**
Stipple the cake board with royal icing using a fine sponge. Leave to dry for 2 hours.

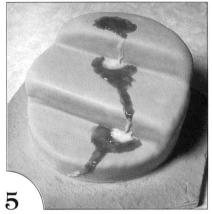

**5**
Colour piping gel as required and spread over the sugarpaste to form a stream.

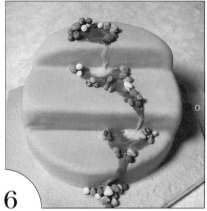

**6**
Make a selection of sugarpaste rocks and fix beside the stream, as shown, using royal icing.

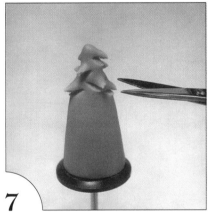

**7**
Make trees by placing a cone shaped piece of sugarpaste onto a flower nail. Cut with scissors to create the branches.

**8**
Fix the trees at the top and base of the cake using royal icing.

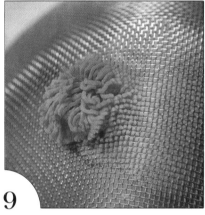

**9**
Push sugarpaste through a wire sieve to form bushes.

**10**
Make various coloured bushes and fix them around the cake as shown.

**11**
Make and fix a variety of sugarpaste flowers and mushrooms then decorate with piping gel.

**12**
Stipple small areas with royal icing and fix in gnome figures. Then decorate with piping gel.

# DUCKY

**1**
Using template as guide, pipe the lines of the duck in royal icing (No.1) onto a dry sugarpaste covered cake.

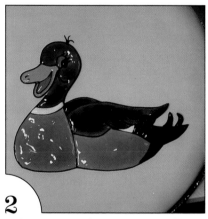

**2**
Colour piping gel as required and fill-in the various parts, as shown.

**3**
Pipe leaves and waves, then fill-in with piping gel.

172

**4**

Tilt the cake and pipe small leaves and flowers, then fill-in with piping gel.

**5**

Pipe inscription of choice, with royal icing, onto the cake-top (No.1).

**6**

Pipe cloud outlines and fill-in with piping gel. Fix a decorative ribbon around the cake board edge.

TEMPLATE

# YULETIDE

**1**

Using a patterned scraper, coat a cake positioned on a cake board, as shown, with royal icing. Leave to dry for 24 hours.

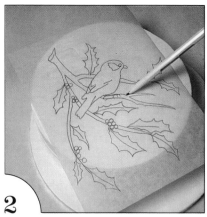

**2**

Transfer the template design onto the cake-top and continue over the side, using a confectioners' pen.

**3**

Using royal icing, pipe over the lines (No.1).

**4**

Using piping gel mixed with various colours, fill-in between the piped lines to form the picture.

**5**

Pipe shells around the cake-base (No.42). Then pipe a dot of piping gel between each shell (No.1). Fix narrow ribbon around the cake-side.

**6**

Using template as guide, pipe YULETIDE (No.1). Then fill-in with piping gel.

TEMPLATES

# RICE PAPER

Rice paper is ideal for decorating cakes of all kinds as it is completely edible as well as being extremely easy to use. It is the perfect medium for anyone who is artistic, and gives tremendous scope for personal creativity, but it can also be used for pretty decorations, such as the flower on page 182, that need no artistic ability at all.

No special tools are required for rice paper as it cuts easily with sharp scissors or a suitable knife. Outlines can either be drawn freehand or around a template. The technique can be adapted for anything from a flat, painted plaque to a more sophisticated, three dimensional shape. Once the basic technique has been mastered, it is easy to create an inexpensive masterpiece with just a little practice.

Flat sheets of rice paper can be purchased from stationers or cake decorating suppliers. The sheets vary in thickness and one side of the paper is smooth while the other has a rougher finish, creating the opportunity for different textures. To avoid damage, the paper should be stored flat in a dry place as it will stick to itself if it becomes damp, and may crack if folded in half.

The primary colours that appeal to children look particularly good on rice paper, but much more subtle colours and delicate shading can be achieved. Rice paper can be easily coloured using a fine paintbrush and piping gel or paste food colours, petal dust etc. When colouring, try to follow the grain of the paper. Too much liquid must be avoided as otherwise the rice paper will wrinkle or disintegrate, but a small amount of water can be used to stick the rice paper to itself. The finished decoration can be attached to the cake top with a tiny amount of royal icing or gel. Rice paper decorations have the advantage of being virtually unbreakable, so they can be easily transported.

Rice paper offers the opportunity for creating your own cake bands, as can be seen from the cake on page 184. This idea could be adapted for children's party cakes by writing the guests' names around the band which, being edible, does not need to be removed before cutting the cake.

As rice paper is such an easy medium to work with, it is ideal for encouraging young children to decorate their own birthday cakes and they may well enjoy reproducing their favourite story book characters.

# PORKY VILLAGE

**1**

Using templates as guide, trace the picture shown onto rice paper with a confectioners' pen.

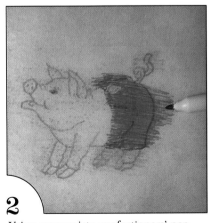

**2**

Using appropriate confectioners' pen colours fill-in the areas, overlapping the outer lines, as shown. Repeat step 1 and 2 for all pictures required.

**3**

When dry, cut-out each picture carefully, leaving a tag at the base to use for plinths.

**4** Place a scalloped card on the cake-top and stipple royal icing around the edge. Then stipple the board.

**5** When stippling is dry, remove the card. Using royal icing, or piping gel, fix the clouds and sun as shown.

**6** Fix the cottages and trees ensuring that the pictures are not obscured too much.

**7** Fix the remaining pictures as shown.

**8** Fix inscription to the front of the cake and decorate with a small ribbon bow.

**9** Pipe shells around the cake-base with royal icing (No.44).

TEMPLATE

Happy Birthday

TEMPLATES

**1** One circle cut from sponge and one sponge bun is required for each head.

**2** Using the sponge size as guide decorate two pieces of rice paper in the design shown.

**3** Place the bun on top of the circle and layer with buttercream, then spread buttercream thinly over the surface. Chill for 1 hour.

**4** Cover the sponge with sugarpaste and place onto the rice paper and cake board.

**5** Cut the face pieces shown, from sugarpaste.

**6** Immediately fix the pieces to the head with cooled, boiled water or egg white.

**7** Carefully melt chocolate over a pan of hot water.

**8** Pour the chocolate into a tall drinking cup and dip a wafer ice-cream cone to cover halfway.

**9** Dip the tip into hundreds and thousands and leave until the chocolate has set.

**10** Fix the cone onto the head and then pipe the hair (No.2).

**11** Brush confectioners' dusting powder onto the cheeks.

**12** Decorate the hat with piped rosettes (No.6) and jelly diamonds.

# LELIA

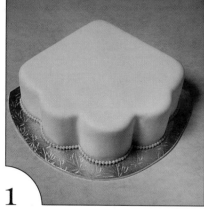

**1**

Cut a cake and board to the shapes shown. Cover the cake with sugarpaste. When dry, pipe shells around the cake-base with royal icing (No.42).

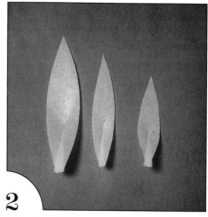

**2**

Using templates as guide, cut petals from rice paper. Snip the base of each petal, moisten with water and overlap to form the shape shown. 30 petals required.

**3**

Carefully moisten and assemble the petals, from the large to the small, to form a lily flower. Leave to dry for 1 hour.

**4** Draw, colour and cut-out lily leaves. Then fix to the cake-top with the flower, using royal icing or piping gel.

**5** Using royal icing, pipe inscription of choice on to the cake-top (Nos.2 and 1).

**6** Pipe tracery around the inscription then decorate cake with ribbon bows.

TEMPLATES

Note: selection of template for use on other cakes

**183**

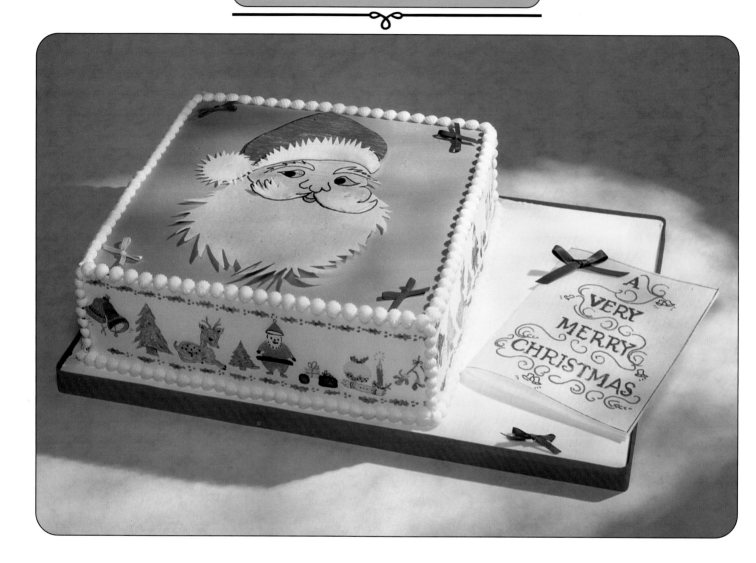

**1**

Follow steps 1 and 2 on page 177 to make the rice paper Father Christmas, card and a cake band to fit around the cake-side.

**2**

Stipple cake board with royal icing and a sponge. When dry, fix cake band to cake-side with royal icing, or piping gel, then pipe shells along the edges to secure (No.43).

**3**

Fix Father Christmas to cake-top with piping gel, then make and fix a ribbon bow on each cake-corner. Place card in position and decorate with bows.

TEMPLATES

# ROYAL ICING

Royal icing is perfect for the elegant lines of formal designs. It produces a sharp, crisp edge for a piped design, or a softer, more flowing line when decorative collars or runouts are used.

With a little practice, it is possible to become proficient in the basic techniques quickly. Instructions are given in the introduction for piping shapes, writing, etc, and practice can be carried out with instant mashed potato on an upturned cake tin until confidence is gained. Always pipe on a coated cake which is thoroughly dry as mistakes can then be scraped off. When making runouts, etc, it is useful to make a few additional ones in case of breakage.

## Timing

Timing is very important when planning a royal iced cake, particularly for an event. A simple wedding cake, like the ones in this book, should be made seven weeks before the wedding to allow three weeks to mature; then one week for covering in almond paste and drying, one week for coating and drying, one week for decoration, with a final week for appreciation or alteration, if required, by the bride. For a birthday cake, allow three weeks for the cake to mature, then almond paste the cake and allow three days to thoroughly dry before coating with royal icing. Then allow a minimum of four days for coating and drying before decoration. The completed cake should then be kept in a cardboard box in a warm dry atmosphere and away from direct sunlight.

## Consistency

The correct consistency of icing for each type of work is important, as is the addition or omission of glycerin. For writing, or piping long lines, the icing needs to be slightly soft as otherwise it will break.

For piping shells or other shapes, however, the consistency needs to be sufficiently stiff to hold its shape with well defined edges and peaks. Flood-in icing has a runny consistency and an easy test is to thin down a small quantity of royal icing and then draw a sharp knife across the top. The line should close up on a count of 7 in warm weather and 10 in colder conditions. Icing for runout and No.1 work should not have glycerin added and should be allowed to stand overnight to allow any bubbles to rise to the surface.

Bowls of icing should be covered with a clean damp cloth to prevent drying out, or should be stored in a closed, food-approved container in a refrigerator. Icing which has been removed from a refrigerator should be allowed to reach room temperature before use. When working, a small amount of icing should be kept in a bowl (covered with a damp cloth if required) separate from the bulk of the icing as this avoids contamination if crystals form. The icing should be kept well scraped down in the bowl to prevent drying out.

## Basic Piped Shapes

When piping it is advisable to use two hands. One hand exerts pressure on the bag whilst the other hand guides the tube. The angle and height of the bag above the cake and the movement of the hands will all help to form the finished shape. The introductory section of this book (pages 40-43) contains detailed instructions for piping all the basic shapes.

If piping is to be over-piped, it is essential to ensure that the previous work is dry enough to support the weight of the additional piping. Scroll borders, which are built up by over-piping several layers, make an extremely effective edging.

## Filigree

This delicate, fill-in technique should be worked in freshly made royal icing without glycerin. Using a fine tube, pipe continuous random loops and whorls as shown on page 231.

## Stippling

Stippling is carried out with a fine, clean sponge or palette knife using icing which will hold its peaks. Roughly spread the icing and gently dab the surface with the sponge or palette knife until the required texture is achieved (see page 160).

## Runouts and Figure Piping

A runout is created by filling in an outline which holds the shape until it dries. Runouts can be used to create elegant collars or decorative motifs. Figure piping, on the other hand, does not have an outline to hold the shape but is piped a little at a time to build up the figure. Templates are given where required for runouts, figures and collars. Templates should be carefully enlarged or decreased according to the size of the cake you are decorating.

To convert royal icing for runout work, fold in sufficient cold water to give a dropping consistency. Before filling the piping bag, tap the container hard to remove bubbles. It is recommended that pure albumen powder be used for the icing. Icing for figure piping needs to hold its shape.

The ideal surface for runout work or figure piping is a glazed tile or a sheet of glass covered with a sheet of waxed paper. If more than one runout is required, these should be made at the same time and allowed to dry together to ensure a uniform finish. Dry runouts should be carefully removed as shown on page 47. Runouts can, however, be piped direct onto the top of the cake. Runouts and piped figures can be stored between sheets of waxed paper in a cardboard box until required.

## Cake Boards

Choosing the correct cake board is vital as the board needs to be strong enough to support the weight of the finished cake, and of the right size and shape for the cake. Fruit cake should always be placed on a 2cm ($1/2$") drum cake board to support the weight.

You will find many ideas in this book for creating unusual cake boards, covering in fabric or lace for instance, and wrapping paper can also create a unique look. Paper covering should be stuck with laundry starch or cornflour whilst fabric can be stuck with special fabric adhesive (care being taken not to mark the fabric or to have any adhesive on the right side of the board). Alternatively, staple to the back of the board. The covering should extend to the back of the board, and the board edge can be covered in ribbon if desired. This should be pinned into place.

## Tiers

Instructions are given on page 27 for tiering a cake and for the appropriate amount of glycerin to add to the icing for each tier of the cake (see page 17).

## Assembly

A tiered cake should always be transported with each tier of the cake in a separate box on the floor of the boot of the car. The cake should then be assembled in its final position.

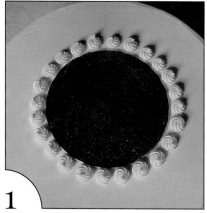

**1** Place a cake card centrally on a dry cake-top. Pipe rosettes beside the cake card, as shown (No.6). Leave to dry, then remove card.

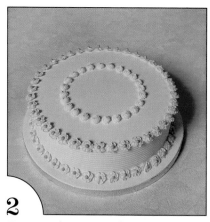

**2** Using royal icing, pipe flowers (see p.44) onto waxed paper (No.57). Leave to dry for 24 hours. 90 required. Fix to the cake-top edge and base with royal icing.

**3** Pipe first letter of inscription in the centre circle (No.2), then complete inscription. Fix a few flowers within the circle to complete decoration.

# FATHER'S DAY

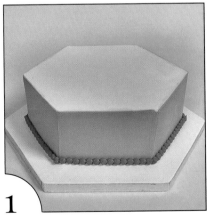

**1**

Coat an hexagonal cake and board with royal icing. Leave to dry for 24 hours. Pipe shells around the cake-base (No.43).

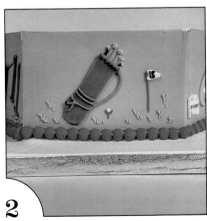

**2**

Using the templates as a guide, cut golf scene from thinly rolled sugarpaste. Fix into place with royal icing and decorate as shown (No.1).

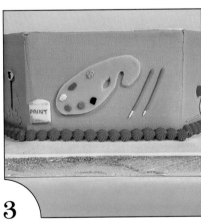

**3**

Using templates as a guide, cut artist's equipment from thinly rolled sugarpaste. Fix into place and decorate as shown (No.1).

**4**

Using the templates as a guide, cut garden scene from thinly rolled sugarpaste. Fix into place and decorate as shown (No.1).

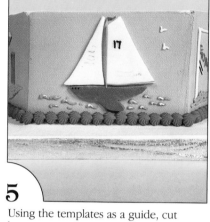

**5**

Using the templates as a guide, cut boating scene from thinly rolled sugarpaste. Fix into place and decorate as shown (No.1).

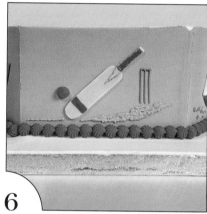

**6**

Using the templates as a guide, cut cricket scene from thinly rolled sugarpaste. Fix into place and decorate as shown (No.1).

**7**

Using the templates as a guide, cut football scene from thinly rolled sugarpaste. Fix into place and decorate as shown (No.1).

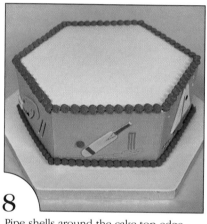

**8**

Pipe shells around the cake-top edge (No.43).

**9**

Using sugarpaste, make and fix several books (see p.136) to the cake-top as shown and then decorate (No.1).

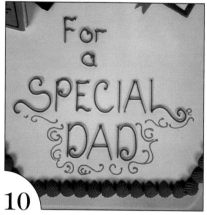

**10**

Pipe inscription of choice below the books and decorate with tracery (No.1).

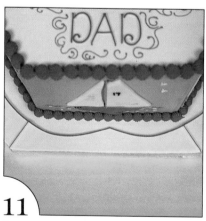

**11**

Pipe a curved line on the cake board, and pipe a straight line from the line to the cake board edge at the corners (No.2).

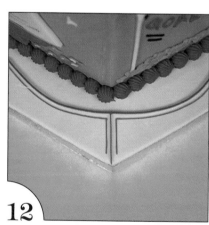

**12**

Pipe a line beside the first line, as shown (No.1).

TEMPLATES

**1**

Coat the cake and cake boards, as shown. When dry, fix ribbon around the edge of each cake board.

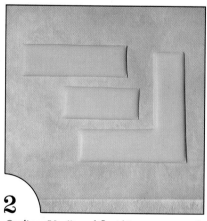

**2**

Outline (No.1) and flood-in runouts and plaques with royal icing, using templates as guide, onto waxed paper (see p.47). Leave to dry for 24 hours.

**3**

Make assorted roses, rose buds and leaves from sugarpaste (see p.48). Leave to dry for 24 hours.

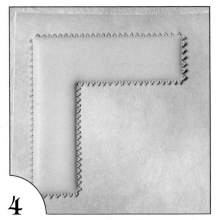

**4**

Pipe dots, to create lace effect around the edge of each corner runout and plaque (No.1).

**5**

Fix the motif to the large plaque. Then pipe the figures onto the small plaque (No.1). Leave to dry for 12 hours.

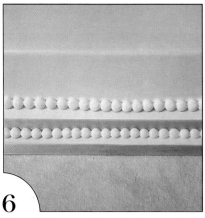

**6**

Pipe shells around the cake-base and first cake board edge (No.3).

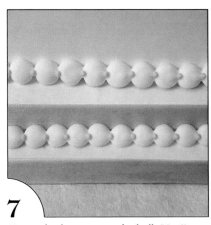

**7**

Pipe a dot between each shell (No.1).

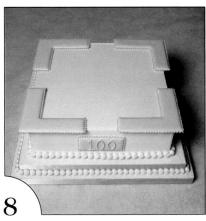

**8**

Remove the runout pieces from the waxed paper and fix to the cake-top and side, as shown, using royal icing.

**9**

Pipe shells along the cake-top edge between the corner runouts (No.3). Then pipe the dots (No.1).

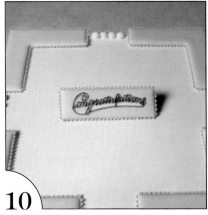

**10**

Fix the centre plaque at an angle as shown, using sugarpaste for support at the back.

**11**

Fix the roses and leaves to form two sprays on the cake-top.

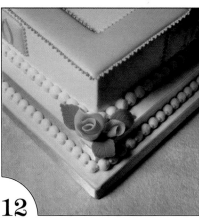

**12**

Fix the roses and leaves to each corner to form sprays, as shown.

TEMPLATES

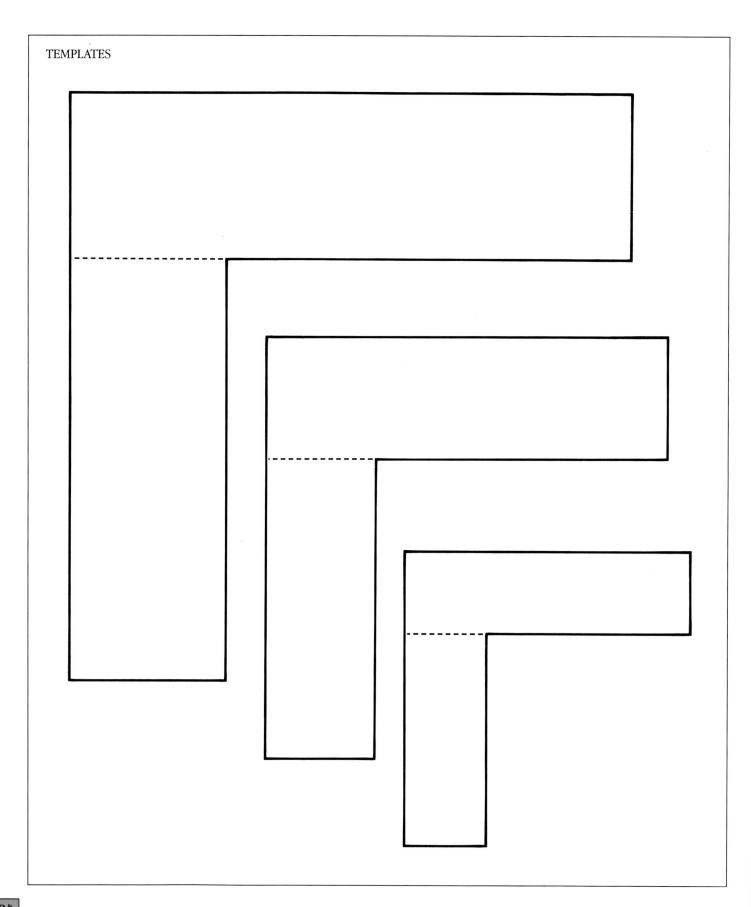

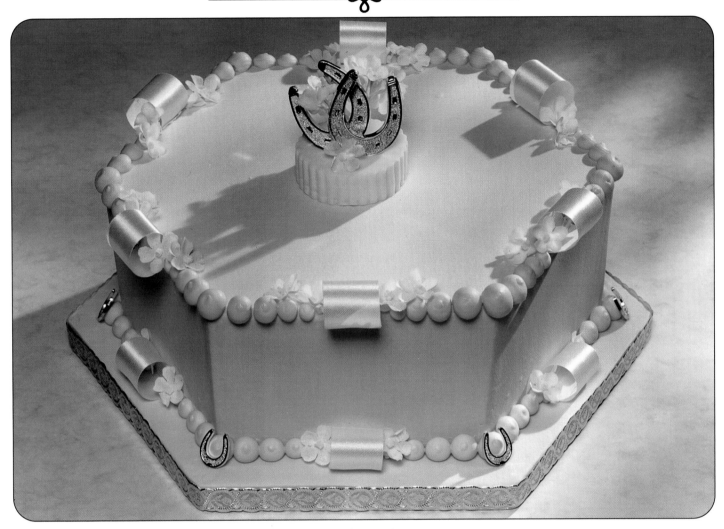

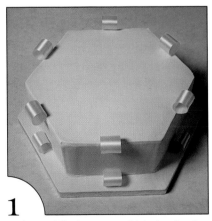

**1**

Make and fix (using royal icing) a food approved ribbon loop on each cake-top edge and base. Leave to dry for 2 hours.

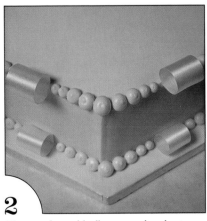

**2**

Pipe graduated bulbs on each cake-top corner and base (No.3).

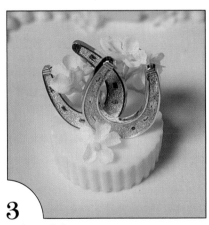

**3**

Make and decorate a sugarpaste centre-piece with horseshoes and flowers. Decorate the cake, as shown in the main picture, with horseshoes and flowers.

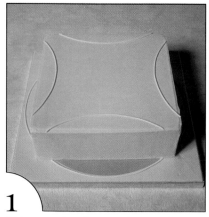

**1**

Using template for a guide, pipe the curved lines onto the cake-top and board using royal icing (No.2). Remove template when icing is dry.

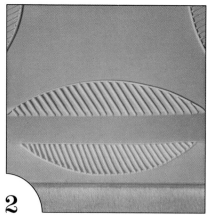

**2**

Pipe straight lines at the angle shown (No.2).

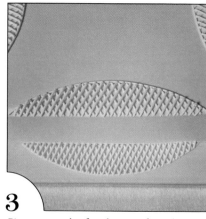

**3**

Pipe across the first lines to form lattice (No.2).

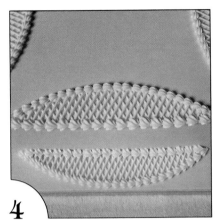

**4**

Pipe shells around the edge of the lattice (No.5).

**5**

Pipe two medium rosettes and one large at each corner of the cake (No.5).

**6**

Pipe inscription of choice (Nos.2 and 1). Finish decoration as required.

TEMPLATES

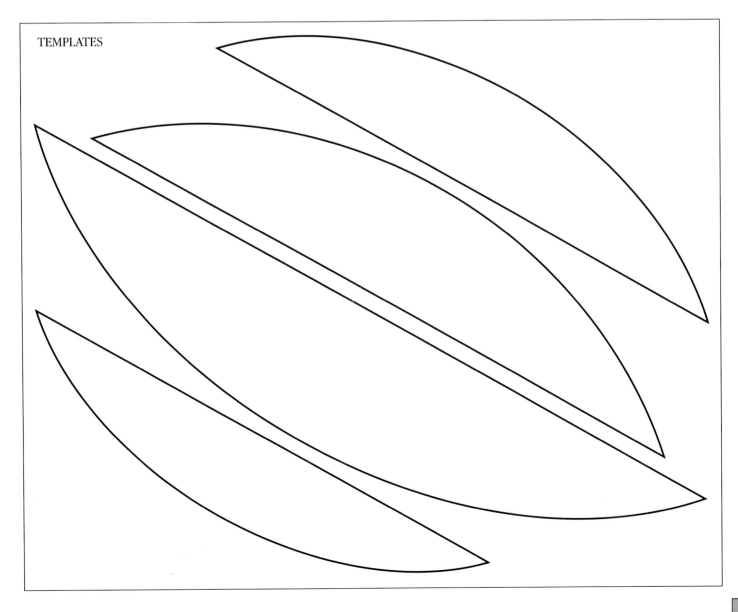

TEMPLATES

**1** Trace templates onto card. Cover with waxed paper and pipe-in ducks (No.4) in the direction of the arrows, using royal icing. 2 large and 20 small required.

**2** Leave to dry for 24 hours. Remove large ducks from paper. Pipe matching design on the reverse sides. Leave to dry for 24 hours. Pipe beak and eyes (No.1).

**3**

Cut flower shapes from sugarpaste.
Indent centres. Pipe stamens (No.1).
Make sugarpaste leaves (see picture 10).

**4**

Coat a 20.5cm (8") round cake on a
28cm (11") board with royal icing (using
a comb scraper to create ripple design
on the board). Leave to dry for
24 hours.

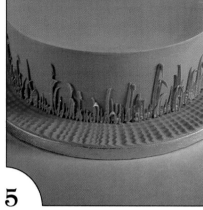

**5**

Pipe long reeds against the cake-side,
using a leaf bag (see p.45).

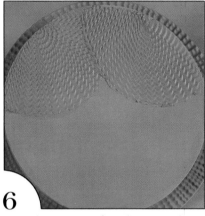

**6**

Spread a quantity of royal icing on the
cake-top and immediately create the
ripple design, using the comb scraper
from step 4.

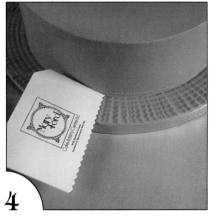

**7**

Fix flowers, leaves and large ducks to
the rippled area.

**8**

Pipe a border of small reeds along the
facing edge of the rippled design (No.1).

**9**

Pipe inscription of choice (No.2). Pipe
the wavy line (No.1).

**10**

Pipe scrolls on the cake-top along the
rippled edge (No.43).

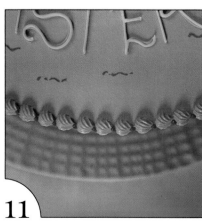

**11**

Pipe shells around the remaining part of
the cake-top edge. Then fix flowers and
ducks around the cake board.

# ZARA

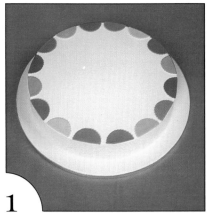

**1** Cut semi-circles of thinly rolled sugarpaste with a crimped cutter. Fix into place on the top-edge of a dry cake and board coated with royal icing.

**2** Make sugarpaste shapes as shown to form body, head and hat.

**3** Fix pieces together with royal icing and decorate as shown (No.1). 16 figures are required.

**4**

Pipe graduated bulbs between each semi-circle (No.2). Fix a crimped circle of sugarpaste to cake-top centre. Fix a stick of rock and decorate with flowers.

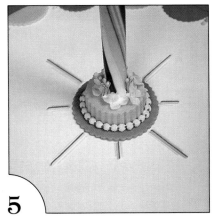

**5**

Pipe shells (No.5), then dots and lines (No.1) around Maypole-base, as shown.

**6**

Fix bodies to the centre of each crimped semi-circle.

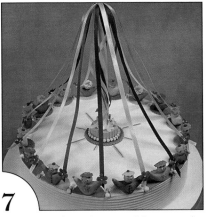

**7**

Fix ribbons from the top of the Maypole to the left hand of each body using a small flower.

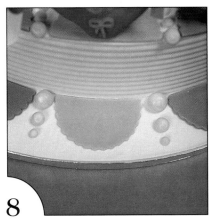

**8**

Cut semi-circles of sugarpaste with a crimped cutter and fix to cake board, as shown. Pipe graduated bulbs between each semi-circle (No.2).

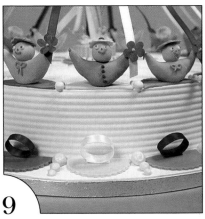

**9**

Make ribbon loops and attach to each semi-circle around cake-base.

**10**

Cut a disc from thin card. Cut a straight line to the centre to form a cone. Fix in place. Pipe inscription of choice (No.1). Leave to dry for 1 hour.

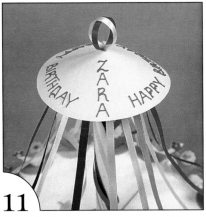

**11**

Carefully fix the cone to the top of the Maypole and decorate centre with ribbon loops.

**12**

Pipe loops around the cone-edge and a dot at each loop-join (No.1).

**1** Cut a square of paper and place on the cake-top centre. Pipe the shells shown (No.42). Leave to dry for 1 hour.

**2** Remove the paper then filigree the centre square and around the cake board edge (No.1).

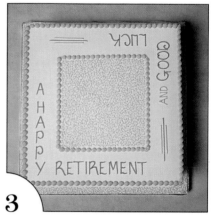

**3** Pipe inscription of choice as shown (No.2). Fix decorations as required.

# JENNIE

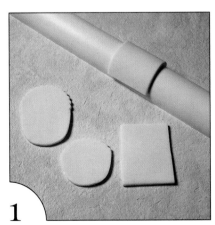

**1**

Using templates as a guide, cut modelling paste into shapes shown. Lay the small oblong over a curve. Leave to dry for 48 hours.

**2**

When dry fix the pieces together, using royal icing, to make the cradle. Leave to dry for 2 hours.

**3**

Make sugarpaste pillow and cover, fix into the cot with baby as shown.

**4**

Decorate the cradle with piped dots (No.1) and a ribbon bow.

**5**

Pipe bulbs around the cake-top edge (No.3).

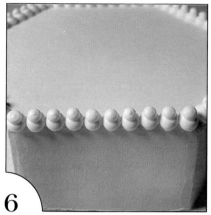

**6**

Pipe a smaller bulb onto each bulb (No.3).

**7**

Repeat steps 5 and 6 around the cake-base.

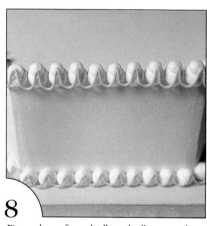

**8**

Pipe a loop from bulb to bulb around the cake-top edge and base (No.2).

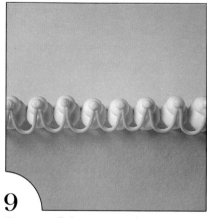

**9**

Pipe a small dot covering the join on each curve (No.1).

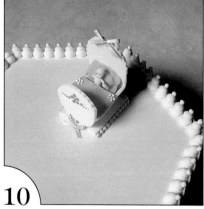

**10**

Fix the cradle onto the cake-top in the position shown. Decorate the cradle base with piped shells (No.1) and a ribbon bow.

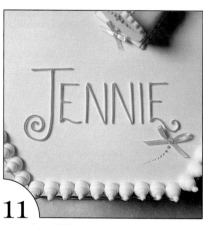

**11**

Pipe the child's name in the design shown (Nos.2 and 1). Decorate with dots and a ribbon bow.

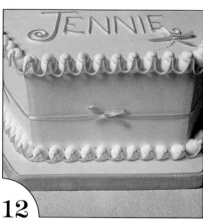

**12**

Fix ribbon and bows around the cake-side. Then fix ribbon around the cake board to complete the cake.

TEMPLATES

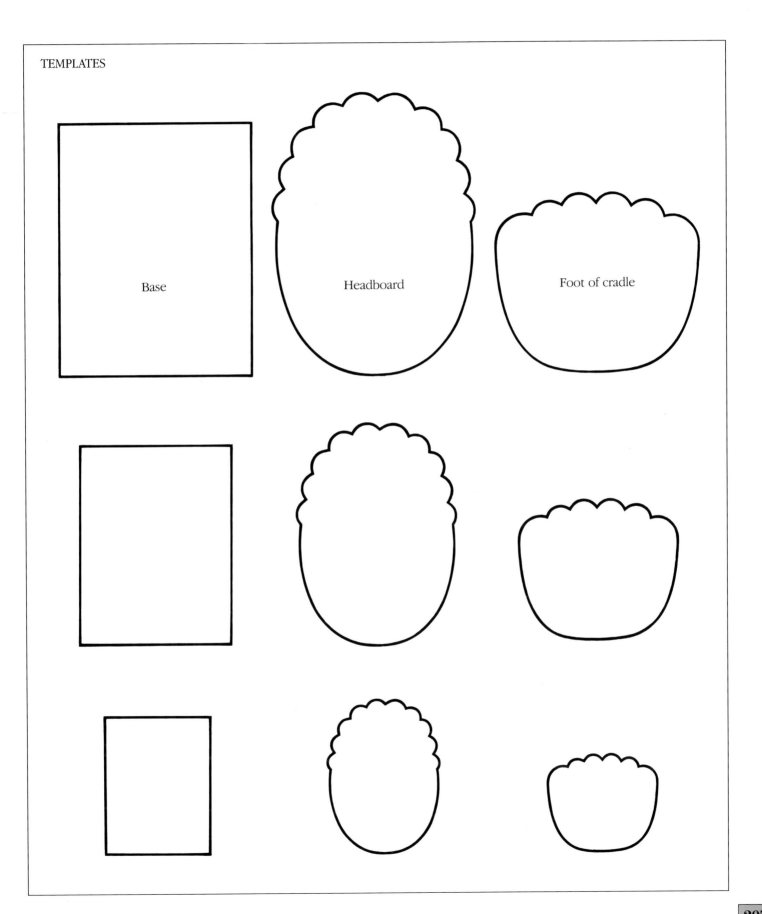

Base

Headboard

Foot of cradle

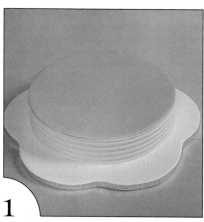

**1**

Coat a 20.5cm (8") round cake and place on a 30.5cm (12") shaped board. (Use a comb scraper on the cake-side.) Flood-in the cake board. Leave to dry for 24 hours.

**2**

Trace Leo's template onto card. Place waxed paper over the template and pipe the lines using royal icing without glycerin (No.1).

**3**

Flood-in the head and body. Leave to dry for 24 hours. Paint features with edible food colouring.

**4**

Divide the cake-top into 12 sections and pipe straight lines to the cake-centre. Pipe signs of zodiac around the cake-edge in piped boxes (No.1).

**5**

Pipe shells around the cake-base (No.2). Then pipe a line on each shell (No.1).

**6**

Pipe the names of the zodiac on the cake board (beneath the appropriate sign) and Happy Birthday under Leo (No.1). Fix Leo to the cake-top.

TEMPLATES

THE ZODIAC

♈ ARIES
♉ TAURUS
♊ GEMINI
♋ CANCER
♌ LEO
♍ VIRGO
♎ LIBRA
♏ SCORPIO
♐ SAGITTARIUS
♑ CAPRICORN
♒ AQUARIUS
♓ PISCES

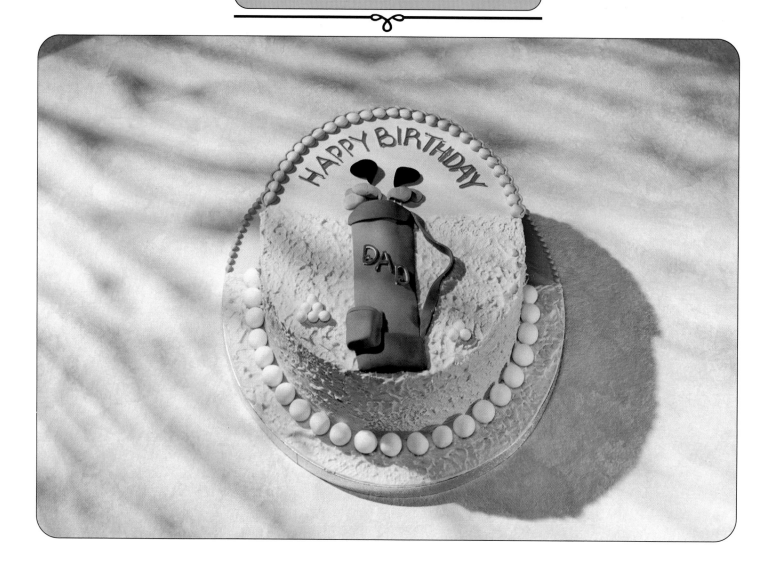

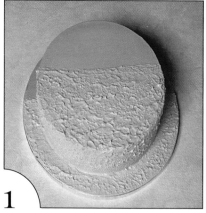

**1** Spread half the cake with green royal icing, as shown, and stipple with a clean dry sponge. Leave to dry.

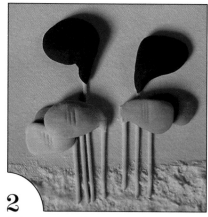

**2** Using the template as a guide, pipe club handles in royal icing (No.2). Then make and fix sugarpaste club heads using royal icing.

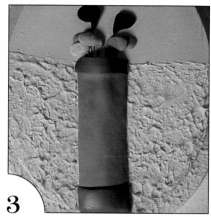

**3** Make and fix a sugarpaste golf bag, and then fix bag edging as shown.

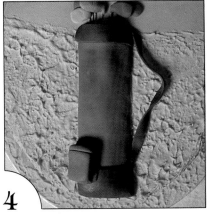

**4**
Make and fix the sugarpaste pocket and
strap.

**5**
Pipe inscription of choice (No.2). Then
overpipe inscription (No.1).

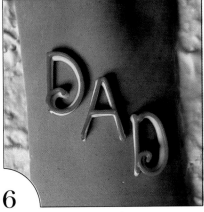

**6**
Pipe name onto the golf bag (No.2).
Then overpipe the name (No.1).

**7**
Pipe shells around the top-edge and
base of the cake (No.3).

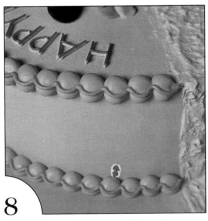

**8**
Pipe a line over each shell (No.2).

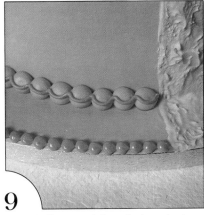

**9**
Pipe shells around the cake board edge
(No.2).

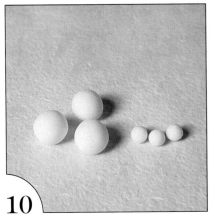

**10**
Make 24 large and 9 small golf balls
from sugarpaste. Leave to dry for
12 hours.

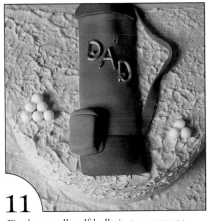

**11**
Fix the small golf balls in two groups,
beside the bag as shown.

**12**
Fix the large golf balls around the
stippled area of the cake-base.

TEMPLATES

**1**

Using template from page 183 as a guide, outline and flood-in whole and half-flower heads. Leave to dry for 24 hours.

**2**

Fix the flowers to the cake-top and base using royal icing, then decorate with piped stems (No.2) and leaves (see p.45).

**3**

Pipe inscription in style shown (No.1). Then pipe skeins around the cake-top edge (No.43). Fix ribbons around cake-side top and cake board edge.

**1** Use a serrated scraper for the final coat on the side of a royal iced cake. Place on doyley and cake board.

**2** Cut fluted discs of sugarpaste. Place on a dry sponge and indent centres with a modelling tool. Leave to dry for 2 hours.

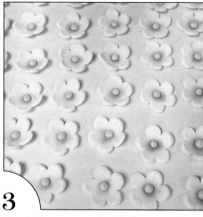

**3** Brush the centre of each flower with confectioners' dusting powder and then pipe a dot of royal icing at the centre (No.1) as shown.

**4** **To make the Teddy Bear:** Mould and fix together with royal icing a sugarpaste body and head as shown.

**5** Mould and fix legs, arms and ears to body and head, to form the Teddy Bear.

**6** Mould and fix the nose. Then pipe the features (No.1). Tie a ribbon bow around neck. Leave to dry for 2 hours.

**7** Pipe shells around cake-base (No.2). Then pipe 'C' scrolls around the cake-top edge (No.7).

**8** Fix the sugarpaste flowers around the cake-base with a dot of royal icing.

**9** Pipe inscription of choice on cake-top (No.2). Over-pipe the inscription (No.1).

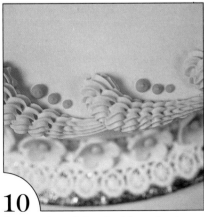

**10** Pipe graduated dots beside each cake-top scroll (No.1).

**11** Decorate the inscription with piped lines and dots (No.1).

**12** Fix the Teddy Bear to the cake-top and position sugarpaste flowers as shown. Pipe grass around the Teddy Bear (No.1). Fix candles and holders as required.

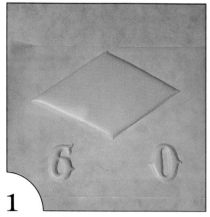

**1**

Using templates as guide, outline and flood-in a diamond and four sets of numerals (see p.47). Leave to dry for 24 hours.

**2**

Pipe shells around the cake-top edge and base, using royal icing (No.44).

**3**

When dry, pipe inscription of choice on the diamond run-out (No.1). Pipe dots around the edge (No.1). Leave to dry for 2 hours.

**4** Fix the diamond run-out onto the cake-top and a set of numerals on each cake-side, using royal icing.

**5** Pipe a dot between each shell (No.1).

**6** Pipe a scalloped rope line beside the shells, as shown (No.1).

TEMPLATES

**1** Lightly moisten the edge of the cake-top with egg white and fix a sugarpaste frill (see p.51) over the side.

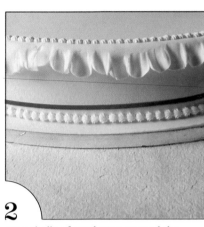

**2** Pipe shells of royal icing around the inside edge of the frill (No.42). Fix a ribbon around the cake-side, then pipe shells around the cake-base.

**3** Fix crystallised flowers (see p.58) with pieces of fern and ribbon loops, to the cake-top, in the position shown. Pipe inscription of choice onto the cake-top (No.2).

**1**

Coat a round cake and board with royal icing in two colours as shown.

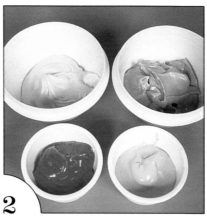

**2**

Colour, in four separate bowls, sufficient royal icing to cover the cake-top.

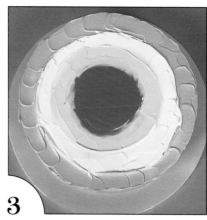

**3**

Spread the four colours on the cake-top as quickly as possible.

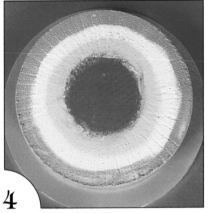

**4**

Immediately stipple the cake-top with a fine sponge so that the colours merge together as shown.

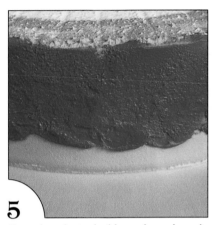

**5**

Spread, and stipple, blue-coloured royal icing around the top of the cake-side to represent the sky.

**6**

Mix three separate colours of sugarpaste and mould to shape shown.

**7**

Place chocolate fingers and flakes around the outside of the sugarpaste to form the bonfire.

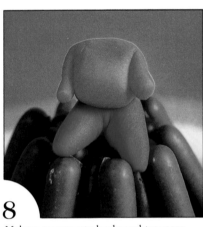

**8**

Make a sugarpaste body and trousers and fix to the top of the fire.

**9**

Make and fix head and hat. Push a chocolate finger into the centre of the bonfire for support. Decorate as shown (No.1).

**10**

Pipe inscription of choice around the fire (No.2). Then overpipe the inscription (No.1).

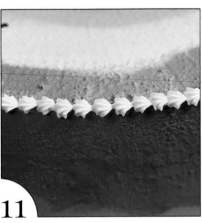

**11**

Pipe shells around the cake-top edge (No.5).

**12**

Make, and decorate, a quantity of sugarpaste cones to represent roman candles, and a pot for 'Penny for the Guy'.

**13**

Fix roman candles around the cake-top.

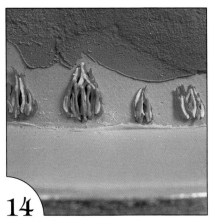

**14**

Pipe bonfires in several colours around the cake-base (No.1).

**15**

Pipe shells below the bonfires around the cake-base (No.2).

**16**

Pipe lines and tracery above bonfires to represent shooting fireworks (No.1).

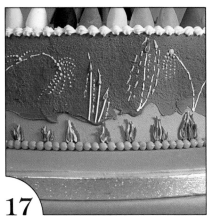

**17**

Pipe dots and dotted lines to illustrate fireworks bursting in the night sky (No.1).

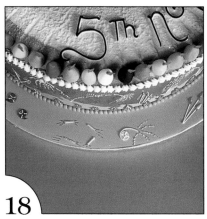

**18**

Pipe a variety of fireworks around the cake board (No.1).

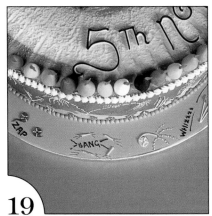

**19**

Pipe firework-noise words between the fireworks on the cake board and decorate with appropriate lines (No.1).

**20**

Fix the 'Penny for the Guy' pot and bundles of chopped chocolate fingers and flake to the cake-top. Fix a colourful ribbon around the cake board edge.

TEMPLATES

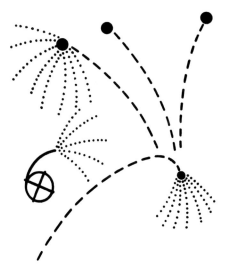

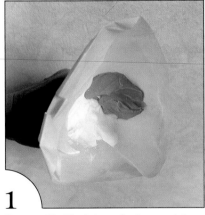

**1** Insert a No.13 piping tube into a piping bag, then fill with two colours of royal icing, as shown.

**2** Pipe shells along the cake-top edge and base keeping the colours in a straight line.

**3** Using pieces of card as a guide (see p.30) pipe inscription of choice (No.2).

**4** Pipe the lines and dots shown (No.2). Then overpipe inscription, lines and dots (No.1).

**5** Pipe a dot between each shell (No.2).

**6** Make and fix an appropriate spray and bow. Then pipe the graduated dots (No.1).

TEMPLATES

**1**

Coat the cake and cake board with royal icing. Leave to dry for 24 hours. Cut a paper template of girl and place onto the cake-top.

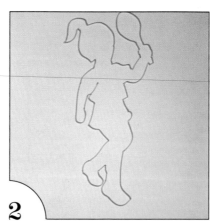

**2**

Pipe a line around the outside of the template (No.1). Leave to dry for 10 minutes.

**3**

Remove template then pipe-in the additional lines shown (No.1).

**4**

Cut flower shapes from sugarpaste, using an appropriate cutter. Fix to cake with royal icing.

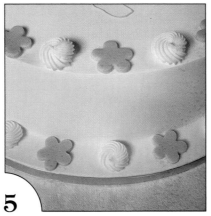

**5**

Pipe a rosette between each flower cut-out (No.13). Repeat around the cake board, placing flowers alternately to the top, as shown.

**6**

Pipe a dot on each rosette (No.2).

**7**

Start to pipe inscription of choice onto the cake-top (Nos.2 and 1). Then underline as shown.

**8**

Pipe remainder of inscription (Nos.2 and 1). Then underline as shown.

TEMPLATE

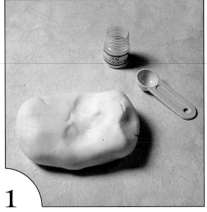

**1**

Make modelling paste (see p.18). Leave covered for 24 hours.

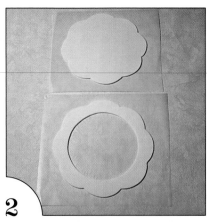

**2**

Cut card template to size required. Using card as guide, cut the modelling paste into two shapes as shown – one solid and one collar. Leave until completely dry.

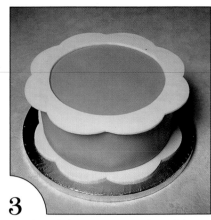

**3**

Fix the solid piece onto the board then the cake. Fix collar onto cake-top, using royal icing. Leave to dry for 2 hours.

**4**

Pipe shells around the edges of both collars (No.2).

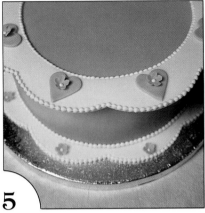

**5**

Make and fix sugarpaste hearts and flowers to the collars, using royal icing. Pipe a dot at each flower centre (No.1).

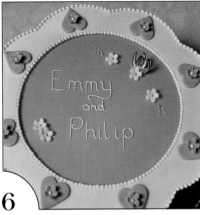

**6**

Pipe inscription of choice onto the cake-top (No.1). Decorate with sugarpaste flowers, piped dots and horseshoes, as shown.

TEMPLATE

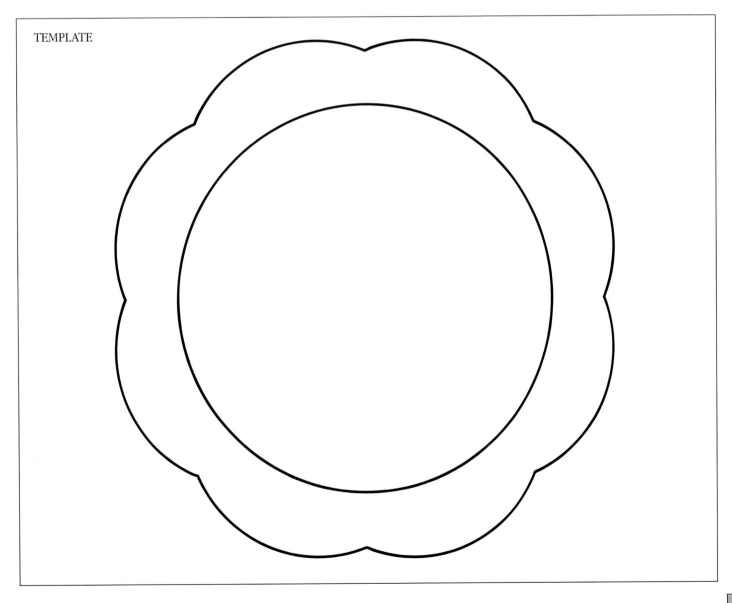

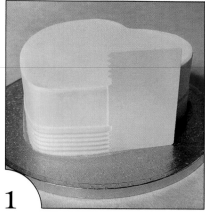

**1** Use a patterned scraper to create the design shown on the cake-side for the final coat of a royal iced cake.

**2** Pipe bulbs around the cake-top edge and base (No.4).

**3** Pipe a scalloped line over the bulbs (No.3).

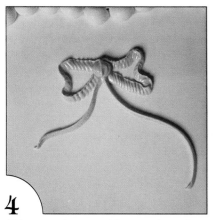

**4**

Using template as guide, scratch-mark the bow onto the cake-top then pipe over as shown (No.57).

**5**

Pipe inscription of choice between the bow tails, as shown (No.1).

**6**

Pipe a spike between each cake-base shell (No.2).

TEMPLATES

**1**

Fix banding around board. Cut a wide ribbon twice the circumference of cake. Gather around the cake-base and secure ends.

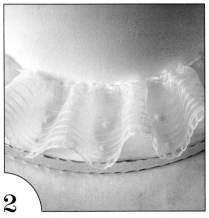

**2**

Arrange the frill in even curves. Pipe a dot in royal icing (No.1) beneath each downturn to secure, then pipe dots onto the ribbon as shown.

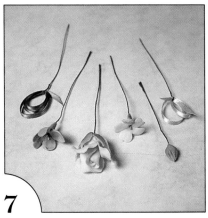

**3**

Pipe shells around the cake-top and cake-base (No.7). Pipe a line of dots beneath the cake-top shells, then above the cake-base shells (No.1).

**4**

Fix four narrow ribbons evenly spaced around the cake-side.

**5**

To make a finger loop wind ribbon around finger and hold with thumb.

**6**

Wind two more loops, increasing size of each loop as shown, then secure with 28 gauge wire and twist. Cut ends and gently pull loops apart.

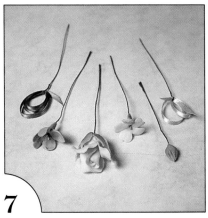

**7**

Use artificial flowers or make a selection of flowers and buds, from flower paste (see p.50 and 115) and finger loops in toning colours.

**8**

Arrange and fix finger loops around a half-rose, as shown. Add more flowers, buds and finger loops to make a full posy.

**9**

Gather ½ metre of ribbon and secure to back of posy. Trim and tape all the wires to complete the top decoration.

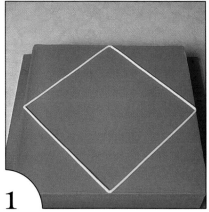

**1**
Place a square card onto the cake-top in the position shown. Pipe a line beside the square (No.4). Leave to dry for 20 minutes then remove the square.

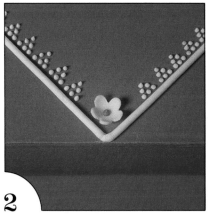

**2**
Fix a flower at each corner, using royal icing, and then pipe dots to form triangles (No.1).

**3**
Pipe filigree over the four corners of the cake-top (No.1).

**4**
Pipe the shape shown onto the cake-top edge (No.6), then repeat the design along one side of the cake-top edge.

**5**
Continue piping around the cake-top edge, keeping the same number of piped shapes for each side.

**6**
Repeat steps 4 to 5 around the cake-base, with the same piping tube.

**7**
Fix a selection of sugarpaste flowers to each cake-side, using royal icing.

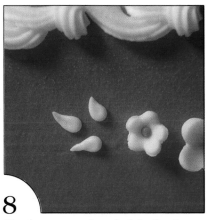

**8**
Pipe leaves at each end of the floral sprays (No.1).

**9**
Fix a horseshoe and sugarpaste flower to each corner. Then pipe the leaves as shown (No.1).

**1**

Make a paper template (see p.28), to shape shown, and place on cake-top with a cake card to hold down. Make and fix a paper template for the cake-side.

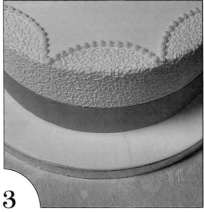

**2**

Pipe shells beside the template, with royal icing (No.42). Leave to dry for 2 hours.

**3**

Carefully remove the top card and template. Pipe filigree as shown (No.1). Leave to dry for 1 hour.

**4**

Carefully remove the paper band. Pipe shells around the middle of the cake-side (No.42) along the edge of the filigree.

**5**

Pipe shells around the cake-base (No.42).

**6**

Pipe filigree around the cake board edge (No.1).

**7**

Pipe shells around the cake board edge (No.42).

**8**

Make and fix ribbons and ribbon bows (as also shown in the main picture) on the cake-top edge and sides.

**9**

Fix matching rose sprays to each tier.

**1**

Using templates as guide, outline and flood-in four double hearts for each tier (see p.47). Leave to dry for 24 hours then decorate as shown (No.1).

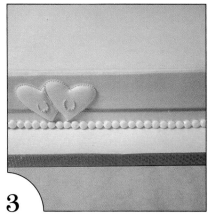

**2**

Crystallise an assortment of freesia flower (see p.58). Leave to dry.

**3**

Fix ribbon around the cake-side and board, then fix a heart to each cake-side. Pipe shells around the cake-base (No.3).

**4**

Fix flowers, horseshoe and ribbon bow with royal icing, as shown.

**5**

Pipe shells on remaining cake-top edge (No.3). Decorate centre of cake with a vase of freesias.

TEMPLATES

**1**

Pipe shells (No.3) around the cake-top edge and base of cakes coated with royal icing. Then pipe a line onto each shell (No.2).

**2**

Using template as guide (see p.28) pipe a petal shaped line onto the cake-top and board (No.2).

**3**

Make a band, from the bridesmaids' dress material, and fit around the cake-side. Gather ends, stitch together and fix.

**4**

Cut and fold a rectangular piece of material, right sides facing. Stitch around side leaving 5cm (2") for turning.

**5**

Turn right side out. Stuff lightly with wadding and stitch to close gap.

**6**

Wrap a narrow band around the rectangle to form a bow. Stitch at the back to secure. Fix bow to ribbon join, using double sided sticky tape.

**7**

Repeat steps 3 to 6 for second tier. Fix a band around edge of each cake board.

**8**

Fill a pillar with sugarpaste. Then make and fix an arrangement of silk flowers, leaves and bows.

**9**

Make two silk floral sprays, as shown. Position on bottom tier and cake board.

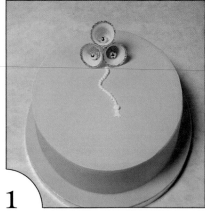

**1**

Fix three large bells to the top of a coated oval cake, using royal icing. Pipe a rope line (No.42).

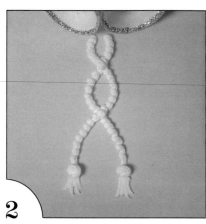

**2**

Pipe a second rope line to form criss-cross pattern (No.42).

**3**

Pipe Noël each side of the bell, at the angle shown (No.1). Decorate with lines (No.1).

**4** Pipe remaining part of message and musical notes (No.1).

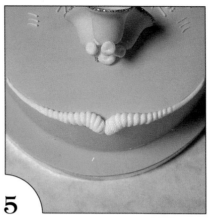

**5** Pipe scrolls at the centre-top of the cake (No.43).

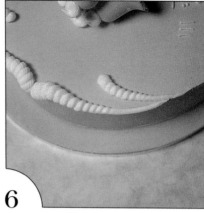

**6** Pipe 'C' scrolls, as shown (No.43).

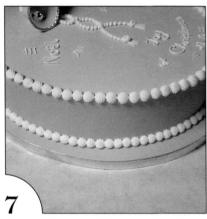

**7** Pipe shells around the remaining cake-top edge and around the cake-base (No.43).

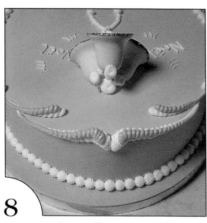

**8** Overpipe the scrolls (No.3).

**9** Pipe a dot between each shell (No.2).

**10** Overpipe the scrolls (No.2).

**11** Fix one wide and two narrow ribbons around the cake-side as shown.

**12** Stipple the cake board edge with royal icing, using a clean sponge, then fix ribbon around board.

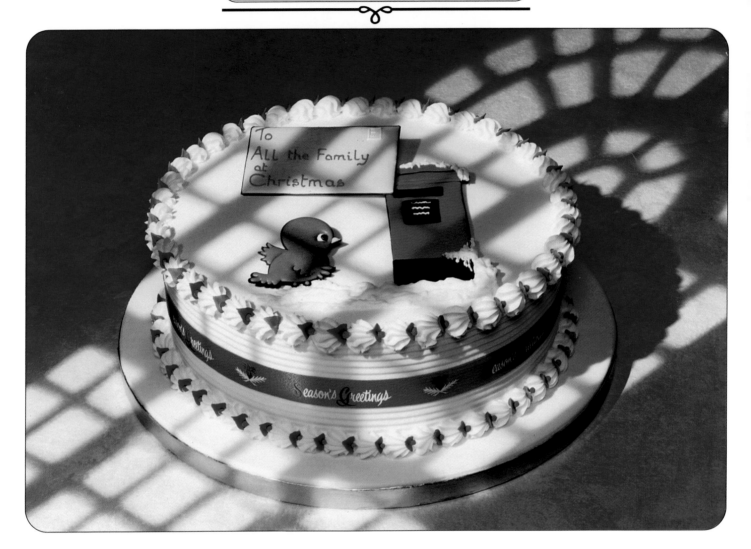

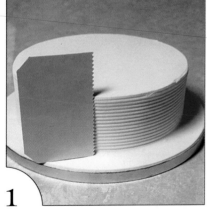

**1**

Use a combed shape scraper to create the pattern shown around the cake-side.

**2**

Using templates as guide, pipe royal icing designs (see p.47) onto waxed paper (No.1). Leave to dry for 2 hours.

**3**

Flood-in the various designs with run-out royal icing. Leave to dry for 24 hours.

**4** Decorate the run-outs and fix onto the cake-top with stippled royal icing to form snow effect.

**5** Pipe shells around the cake-top edge and base (No.13).

**6** Pipe a leaf, using a leaf bag (see p.45), between each shell then pipe a berry (No.1).

TEMPLATES

241

# CHRISTMAS

**1** Coat a cake using a combed scraper around the side.

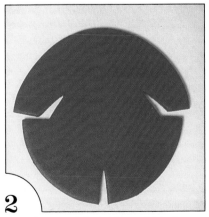

**2** Cut, shape and fix (with royal icing) a sugarpaste disc to the cake-top, using template as a guide.

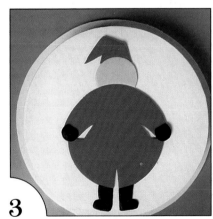

**3** Cut and fix the further sugarpaste shapes as shown, using the template as a guide.

**4** Decorate Father Christmas using royal icing (No.42). Then fix sugarpaste eyes, nose and buttons.

**5** Roll out, cut and fix sugarpaste trees to the cake-side, using template as guide. Pipe snow as shown (No.2).

**6** Pipe message of choice (No.1). Pipe shells around the cake-top edge as shown (No.43). Make and fix a sugarpaste sack and ribbon bow.

TEMPLATES

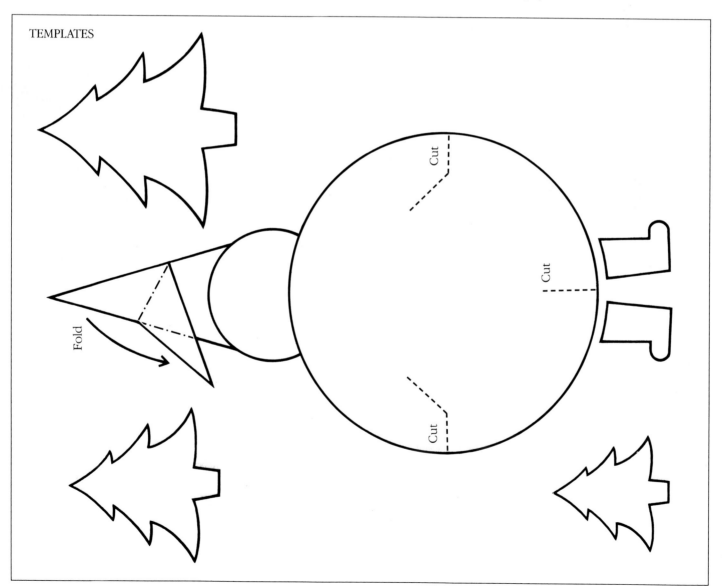

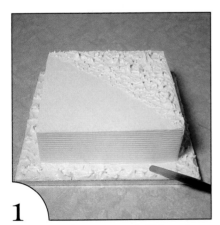

**1**
Stipple royal icing across half the cake-top and then around the cake board, using a small palette knife. Leave to dry for 2 hours.

**2**
Pipe scrolls along the cake-top edge as shown (No.44).

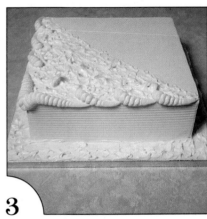

**3**
Pipe further scrolls along the cake-top edge as shown (No.44).

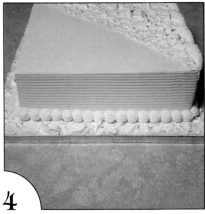

**4**

Pipe shells around the cake-base
(No.44).

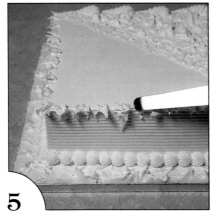

**5**

Stipple the remaining cake-top edges
with royal icing to form icicles.

**6**

Overpipe each scroll (No.3).

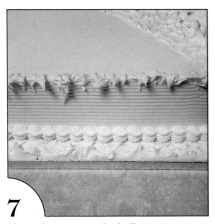

**7**

Pipe a line over each shell (No.2).

**8**

Overpipe all the piping (No.1).

**9**

Pipe a spike at the join of each shell
(No.2).

**10**

Pipe message of choice onto the cake-
top (No.1).

**11**

Decorate the message with piped lines
and stippled snow.

**12**

Fix decorations on the cake-top and
sides, then fix a ribbon around the cake
board.

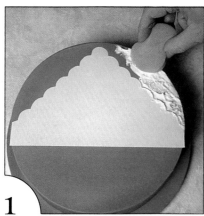

**1**

Cut a card template, to the shape shown, and place onto a dry cake covered surface. Stipple with royal icing as shown to represent snow.

**2**

Cut a scalloped template pattern for the side, and stipple. Then stipple the cake board.

**3**

Using template as a guide, cut sugarpaste bells and place onto the cake-top, raising the middle with a piece of sugarpaste to form a dome.

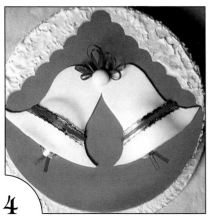

**4** Decorate the bells with ribbons and bows.

**5** Pipe inscription of choice (No.1). Fix centre bow with royal icing.

**6** Pipe musical notes around the cake-base (No.1). Then fix ribbon around cake board edge.

TEMPLATES

# SWEETIE

**1**

Coat a cake in royal icing and leave to dry for 24 hours. Then stipple with royal icing as shown, using a clean dry sponge.

**2**

Fix two rows of sugar coated chocolate sweets around the cake-sides.

**3**

Make and fix sugarpaste trees (see p.171) on the cake-top and board. Then place card in centre. Fix ribbon around the board edge. Fix bow to cake-top.

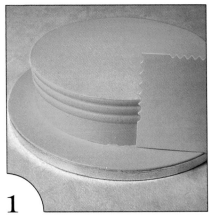

**1** Coat the cake and board in two coats of royal icing. Then use a patterned scraper on the cake-side on the final coat. Leave to dry for 24 hours.

**2** Place doyley onto cake-top. Spread icing (slightly softened with water) thinly. When covered and smooth, immediately peel doyley off cake-top in one continuous movement.

**3** Pipe shells around the cake-base (No.43). Decorate cake with sugarpaste holly and berries.

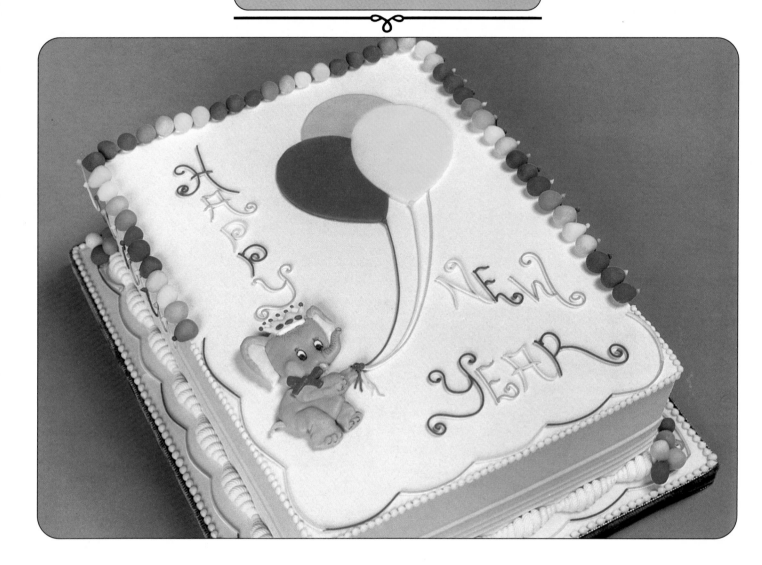

TEMPLATE

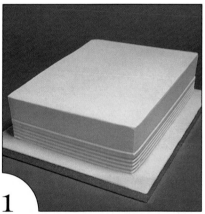

**1**

Coat an oblong cake in royal icing. Use a patterned scraper to create the effect shown. Then coat the board.

**2**

Cover template with waxed paper. Pipe-in the parts shown with royal icing.

**3**

Continue to pipe-in the further parts as shown.

**4**

Complete piping remaining parts as shown. Leave to dry for 24 hours. Brush-in eyes and the markings shown with edible food colouring.

**5**

Roll brightly coloured sugarpaste into balloons for cake-edge.

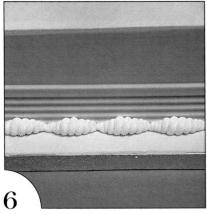

**6**

Pipe spiral shells around the cake-base (No.43).

**7**

Carefully remove elephant from waxed paper and fix in place. Form three balloons from sugarpaste. Fix into place and pipe strings (No.1).

**8**

Pipe inscription of choice on the cake-top (No.1). Fix sugarpaste balloons around part of the cake-top edge.

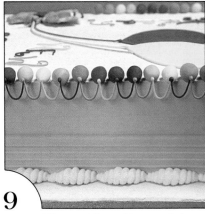

**9**

Pipe a different coloured loop to link each balloon (No.1). Then pipe a dot at each loop join.

**10**

Pipe and overpipe, curved lines and shells on the cake-top edge (Nos.2 and 1).

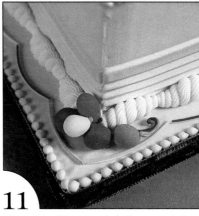

**11**

Pipe curved lines and shells around the cake board edge (No.1). Then fix balloons to each corner.

# INDEX AND GLOSSARY

**Cake-base. Where the bottom edges of the cake meet the cake board.**

**Cake card. Thin cake board**

**Coated cake. A cake coated in buttercream or royal icing.**

**Colouring**
**– Buttercream. Mix colour into the buttercream after it has been made.**
**– Flower paste. Fold and mix the colour into the paste.**
**– Granulated sugar. Carefully add edible food colouring to the sugar, mix thoroughly. Allow to dry for 24 hours.**
**– Marzipan or almond paste. Fold and mix colour into the marzipan.**
**– Partial mix. Where colouring is not fully mixed into the medium used.**
**– Piping gel. Stir the colour into the gel.**
**– Royal icing. Mix colour into the royal icing after it has been made.**
**– Sugarpaste. Fold and mix the colour into the paste.**

**Covered cake. A cake covered in almond paste or sugarpaste.**

**Fix. To join**
– Use apricot puree when fixing cake to cake or marzipan to cake.
– Use cooled boiled water or clear liquor when fixing sugarpaste to sugarpaste.
– Use royal icing when fixing to royal icing.
– Use royal icing when fixing run-outs, or piped figures, to royal icing or sugarpaste.

*Fix to join continued*
– Fix sugarpaste to buttercream by pressing it gently into the buttercream.
– Fix artifical decorations to sugarpaste, or royal icing, with royal icing.
– Fix ribbons – see p.81.

**Flood-in – see Outline.**

**Gum Arabic Solution:** Boil 85g (3oz) of water. Remove from heat and immediately whisk in 30g (1oz) of gum arabic powder. Leave to cool. Remove any surface film and store in a refrigerator until required.

# PIPING TUBE SHAPES

The diagram shows the icing tube shapes used in this book. Please note that these are Mary Ford tubes, but comparable tubes may be used. All the tools and equipment required to complete the cakes and decorations in this book are obtainable from the Mary Ford Cake Artistry Centre, 28-30 Southbourne Grove, Bournemouth, Dorset BH6 3RA, England or from local stockists.

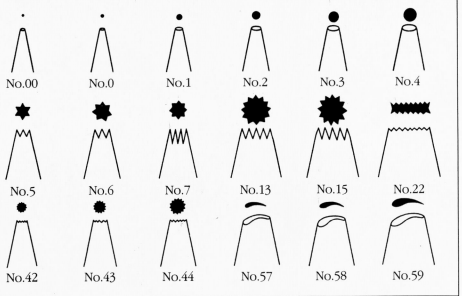

No.00  No.0  No.1  No.2  No.3  No.4

No.5  No.6  No.7  No.13  No.15  No.22

No.42  No.43  No.44  No.57  No.58  No.59

### 101 Cake Designs

ISBN: 0 946429 00 6      320 pages
The original Mary Ford definitive cake artistry text book. A classic in its field, over 250,000 copies sold.

### Cake Making and Decorating

ISBN: 0 946429 41 3      96 pages
Mary Ford divulges all the skills and techniques cake decorators need to make and decorate a variety of cakes in every medium.

### Chocolate Cookbook

ISBN: 0 946429 18 9      96 pages
A complete introduction to cooking with chocolate featuring sweets, luscious gateaux, rich desserts and Easter Eggs.

### Jams, Chutneys and Pickles

ISBN: 0 946429 33 2      96 pages
Over 70 of Mary Ford's favourite recipes for delicious jams, jellies, pickles and chutneys with hints and tips for perfect results.

### Suparpaste Cake Decorating

ISBN: 0 946429 10 3      96 pages
27 innovative Mary Ford cake designs illustrating royal icing decoration on sugarpaste covered cakes.

### Children's Cakes

ISBN: 0 946429 35 9      96 pages
33 exciting new Mary Ford designs and templates for children's cakes in a wide range of mediums.

### Party Cakes

ISBN: 0 946429 09 X      120 pages
36 superb party time sponge cake designs and templates for tots to teenagers. An invaluable prop for the party cake decorator.

### Sugar Flowers Cake Decorating

ISBN: 0 946429 12 X      96 pages
Practical, easy-to-follow pictorial instructions for making and using superb, natural looking sugar flowers for cakes.

### Decorative Sugar Flowers for Cakes

ISBN: 0 946429 28 6      120 pages
33 of the highest quality handcrafted sugar flowers with cutter shapes, background information and appropriate uses.

### Sugarcraft Cake Decorating

ISBN: 0 946429 30 8      96 pages
A definitive sugarcraft book featuring an extensive selection of exquisite sugarcraft items designed and made by Pat Ashby.

### Making Glove Puppets

ISBN: 0 946429 26 X      96 pages
14 specially designed fun glove puppets with full size templates and step-by-step instructions for each stage.

### Home Baking with Chocolate

ISBN: 0 946429 37 5      96 pages
Over 60 tried and tested recipes for cakes, gateaux, biscuits, confectionery and desserts. The ideal book for busy mothers.

### Desserts

ISBN: 0 946429 40 5      96 pages
Hot and cold desserts suitable for every occasion using fresh, natural ingredients. An invaluable reference book for the home cook, student or chef.

### The Complete Book of Cake Decorating

ISBN: 0 946429 36 7      256 pages
An indispensable reference book for cake decorators, containing totally new material covering every aspect of cake design and artistry.